D0021870

*An Education
for
Our Time*

An Education for Our Time

JOSIAH BUNTING III

REGNERY PUBLISHING, INC.
Washington, D.C.

Copyright © 1998 by Josiah Bunting III

All rights reserved. No part of this publication may be reproduced or transmitted in any form or by any means electronic or mechanical, including photocopy, recording, or any information storage and retrieval system now known or to be invented, without permission in writing from the publisher, except by a reviewer who wishes to quote brief passages in connection with a review written for inclusion in a magazine, newspaper, or broadcast.

Library of Congress Cataloging-in-Publication Data

Bunting, Josiah, 1939–
    An education for our time / Josiah Bunting III
       p.   cm.
    ISBN 0-89526-369-6 (alk. paper)
    I. Title.
    PS3552.U48E38 1998
    813'.54—DC21   98-24842
                                                     CIP

Published in the United States by
Regnery Publishing, Inc.
An Eagle Publishing Company
One Massachusetts Avenue, NW
Washington, DC 20001

Distributed to the trade by
National Book Network
4720-A Boston Way
Lanham, MD 20706

Printed on acid-free paper.
Manufactured in the United States of America

10 9 8 7 6 5 4 3

Books are available in quantity for promotional or premium use. Write to Director of Special Sales, Regnery Publishing, Inc., One Massachusetts Avenue, NW, Washington, DC 20001, for information on discounts and terms or call (202) 216-0600.

To Lewis Lapham

CONCORDIA UNIVERSITY LIBRARY
PORTLAND, OR 97211

DONGGUK UNIVERSITY LIBRARY

Contents

There is no need to suppose that
human beings differ very much one
from another: but it is true that
the ones who come out on top are
the ones who have been trained in
the hardest school.

Thucydides
The Peloponnesian War, 1,1.84.4

Foreword

by William J. Bennett

MAJOR GENERAL JOSIAH BUNTING III was not given an easy task in June of 1996. Although he had served as president of several universities, he was about to embark on his most challenging assignment of all: integrating women into the previously all-male Virginia Military Institute (VMI). While he disagreed with the Supreme Court's decision declaring such institutions unconstitutional—and fought it zealously—he accepted it. And he changed the university, accommodating it to the new cadets while preserving many of the traditions that had made VMI what it was.

In our day—when faced with demands for "new" history, quotas for literature, gender equality, affirmative action, and women's studies—we see that times are changing in American higher education. But General Bunting was responsible for changing within a year an institution that had gone more than 150 years without much change. He understood that conservatism is not about dogmatic opposition. It is, as Abraham Lincoln said, about preserving the best of the past.

Yet this book is the tale not of Bunting's personal or political struggles but rather of his ongoing exploration of timeless truths about education. He writes that "the business of undergraduate education remains the cultivation of character and mind, of instinct and ability, of leadership and service. It is the way men should live and behave in our culture and our country that is the proper business of our colleges."

Reading such passages, I was reminded of my tenure at the United States Department of Education. In 1988 I gave a speech at Stanford University in which I responded to growing, hostile arguments for something called "Cultures, Ideas, and Values," a new curriculum meant to replace Stanford's Western Civilization program.

Here's part of what I said then:

> The point for contemporary higher education is this. The classics of Western philosophy and literature amount to a great debate on the perennial questions. To deprive students of this debate is to condemn them to improvise their ways of living in ignorance of their real options and the best arguments for each. Consider the point/counterpoint of Western thought. On the ends of government, whom do we follow—Madison or Marx? On the merits of the religious life—Aquinas or Voltaire? On the nobility of the warrior—Homer or Erasmus? On the worth of reason—Hegel or Kierkegaard? On the role of women—Wollstonecraft or Schopenhauer? The study of Western civilization is not, then, a case for ideology; it is a case for philosophy and thoughtfulness. It considers not only the one hand, but the one hand and the other—and, just as often, the third and fourth hands as well. Those who take the study of the West seriously end up living a variety of different lives and arriving at a diversity of opinions and

positions. And for this diversity, in the West as nowhere else, there is unparalleled tolerance and encouragement.

I cite that speech in order to prepare the reader for Bunting's radical task. General Bunting wants to show us how—that is, *in what manner* and *by what means*—we might resuscitate the serious study of fundamental, permanent human questions. He wants to show how we might expand students' minds by refining their field of inquiry—how we might deepen their souls by locating, and then cultivating, their better angels.

For many years, conservatives, and even some liberals, have raised concerns about the American higher-education system. Indeed, most of us now know the failings, the scandals, the problems, and even the causes of the problems. But Josiah Bunting does not just criticize; he has moved beyond the merely descriptive to the prescriptive and the constructive. He provides a glimpse of a "new and improved" American higher-education system ("new and improved" though it stems from the successes the past) and shows how that improved education might lead to better citizens and how these better citizens might lead to a better nation.

General Bunting presents an outline of an ideal university, organizing it around the answers to five specific questions he presents early on:

1. What is our mission?
2. Who should our students be?
3. How should they live?
4. What should they learn?
5. Who should lead and teach them?

Of course, these are the same questions that were asked by Plato and Aristotle. Bunting's answers thus, quite properly, point back (and up) to the ancients, the classics. We should teach our students to be virtuous—to be rugged, responsible individuals, as well as faithful, dedicated citizens. Teaching students a specific technical skill is not as important as teaching them how to think. Nor is it as important as teaching them to be good people. These currently quaint lessons are what guide Josiah Bunting's tenure at VMI. They are what guide this work as well.

George Washington made the relevant point in a letter to his nephew in 1790:

> To point out the importance of circumspection in your conduct, it may be proper to observe that a good moral character is the first essential in a man, and that the habits contracted at your age are generally indelible, and your conduct here may stamp your character through life. It is therefore highly important that you should endeavor not only to be learned but virtuous. Much more might be said to shew the necessity of application and regularity, but when you must know that without them you can never be qualified to render service to your country, assistance to your friends, or consolation to your retired moments, nothing further need be said to prove their utility.

The proper business of our colleges is indeed to form citizens—not simply doctors or lawyers or computer programmers. You wouldn't know it by the numbers. Less than 25 percent of today's undergraduates are liberal-arts majors. Just over 25 percent are business majors; most of the rest follow vocational tracks to fields such as health care and primary and secondary education. Bunting is right: "The things our country requires are simply not the things our colleges are prepared to deliver." We must recover the idea that education is about more than making a living. Education's best claim, William James said, is that it teaches a person to value what deserves to be valued.

And in *The Abolition of Man*, C.S. Lewis writes: "We make men without chests and expect of them virtue and enterprise. We laugh at honor and are shocked to find traitors in our midst." Citizens are so made—with or without hollow chests—through education. The education Bunting provides at VMI, and recommends here, makes citizens with chests.

Pledging our lives, our fortunes, and our sacred honor is not popular at the moment. But it remains as essential now as it did in 1776. And it remains the hallmark of a good citizen, a good American, a good person. Education is about more than knowledge of academic interests. It is about the formation of character. This latter point is the focus, indeed the noble thesis, of Josiah's elegantly written book.

William J. Bennett
May 1998

An Explanatory Note

I AM PLEASED TO SET BEFORE THE READER the description of a new American college.

Groundbreaking is only a few weeks off, the funds are fully committed, and the school will enroll its first class (called a "cohort" in the language of the place) in the fall of the year 2000. My involvement is an odd story.

For three years I have worked at the Virginia Military Institute (VMI), where we have worked to sustain our way of education while complying with the 1996 United States Supreme Court ruling that we enroll female, as well as male, cadets.

But earlier this year, a stranger called me from Chicago. He told me he was the chairman of the board of a new college in Wyoming and asked whether I would consider joining the board. I asked for more information.

Within three weeks I received almost four hundred pages of typescript describing every aspect of the College. With the typescript came an explanatory note from a Mr. Parkman:

…You would be the only academic person on our board, at least at the beginning. The founder did not like academics—

or, rather, thought most of them ill-suited to the kind of education he had in mind. I mentioned your name to him only ten days before he died. He had no idea who you were, but when I mentioned VMI he said (this was on the phone), "Yes, that's good."

The papers attached are copies of his instructions to me. They consist mainly of five long chapters about different aspects of the College, but there are also a few letters—usually written to accompany the chapters as he finished them. For the sake of order and chronology I have enclosed my own brief responses. The man's name was John Adams, and you have no doubt read about his gift in the *New York Times*. It is, by a wide margin, the largest ever made to an American college: $985,000,000.

Read through the papers, won't you? to inform yourself about our project. It occurs to me also that you might want to publish them. We hold the copyright. It would certainly be useful to the College. Do so, if the spirit moves you; we can talk about it at our May meeting. It will be held in Douglas, Wyoming, close to the site, in the foothills of the Laramies.

Mr. Adams's initial call to me was as peremptory as my call, and this letter, to you. But that is often how the best things get done. He needed a tax lawyer. He had once used our firm for other purposes, so he wrote me. Now our board needs what Adams once called a so-called educator, so I have written you. But I sense this kind of work may appeal to you.

I look forward to working with you. The Adams Foundation will pay your expenses, of course, and would obviously underwrite the costs associated with editing and publishing these papers.

Faithfully,

Robert Parkman

Little editing has in fact been necessary. But I should say something about the man Mr. Parkman describes simply as "the founder."

The first thing to say is that what John Adams (1926–1998) wanted us to know about himself and his ideas is in these papers. He liked to use words like apt, effective, functional, purposive. His highest accolade for another was that the person was "able." He made the best of what was set before him; he did not brood or exult. He was interested in *doing*, not in self-advertisement.

His was not a typical CEO kind of life. He hated golf. He despised the culture of Floridian and South Carolinian retirements by the American well-to-do. He was unclubbable. Moreover, he had not been married since 1952, when he had lost his wife Christina to a virulent and rapid leukemia. They hadn't been married long enough to have children. John Adams's solace, as it often is for such men, was his work, his library, and his weekends and summers on the Great Plains.

Mr. Adams was a man of business, but like the best of his generation he believed that acquiring a liberal education was a lifelong endeavor.

He had been an undergraduate at the University of Chicago in the last days of the famous Robert Maynard Hutchins. There is a picture of him the morning after his graduation, standing alongside a 1950 Ford convertible, a rucksack visible on the back seat, a copy of *Oblomov* lying next to it. Adams was on his way to the Ash Hollow region of western Nebraska—to hike, alone. In the picture, he looks little different from the man who appeared on the cover of *Business Week*: short, bandy-legged, reddish-sandy hair, his expression amused and unassuming.

Adams had been badly wounded on Iwo Jima, or he no doubt would have fought in Korea, as well, rather than graduating from Chicago in 1951. He had old-fashioned notions of patriotism, loved the Marines, loved being among them, and loved the America of his time. As he told Mr. Parkman in the fall of 1997, he'd lived through the Great Depression in the old heartland town of Decatur, Illinois; had served in World War II; had rolled up his sleeves in the prosperous Eisenhower years; had served in the Kennedy administration; had lived through the Cold War, Vietnam, the Civil Rights movement, Watergate, the Reagan restoration, and the emergence of America as the *only* superpower. And he had been, as *Forbes* said in an obituary, "Not a major player—a dominant one," in the astounding explosion of information technology after 1980.

John Adams lived quietly, happily, alone. Like Father Hesburgh of Notre Dame, whom he admired above all his contemporaries, he was free to put himself at the service of *pro bono* boards: the orchestra, churches, hospitals, civic organizations, "drives," and universities and colleges. He loved such work. He appears by all accounts to have romanticized his own salad days (at boarding school; at Chicago; and at Clare College, Cambridge, to which the university had sent him for a postgraduate year). But he would, it appears, have been a great college teacher himself, probably at one of those little places he so admired, like Kenyon or Sewanee. He would have flung himself into the work just as he flung himself into everything.

Adams followed John Kennedy to Washington in that brave winter of 1960–61. "Bliss was it in that dawn to be alive, but to be young was very heaven!" There must have been thirty men like him in the suite of the young president—the junior officers of World War II, someone said, now come to power. He was only thirty-five, but the Defense and State Departments were full of brilliant men in their mid- and late thirties, ready, like their leader, to pay any price, bear any burden… to get the country moving again. It was the time of the Peace Corps, the Green Berets, of invigorating certitude about our mission in the world, of fifty-mile marches, late-night Aspen-style seminars about Kant and the *Federalist*. Its infantry (sometimes called Whiz Kids) embraced John Adams, who had already, in barely nine years, made his name at IBM.

He served in the Kennedy administration and remained in the Defense Department for four years after the assassination. At first he worked in Systems Analysis, then all the rage, the premise being that effectiveness in military operations, like effectiveness in anything else, had to be analyzed ruthlessly, objectively, both in terms of costs and results. At the end of 1964 he became a deputy assistant secretary for plans, and for the next thirty months, his last in government, watched the American mission in Vietnam go awry. It was a time of singular lunacies, such as various air operations calculated to "send a message" to Ho Chi Minh, through fine calibrations of destructive forces and syncopated "bombing pauses," which must surely have reduced any serious Hanoi general to helpless mirth. Adams saw this quite clearly, talked to his superiors about it, and to Mr. McNamara once or twice—this is not the way to fight such an enemy; either do it right or don't do it. And then he got out.

There was scarring, and I believe it is visible in Adams's ideal college, as you will read. You may call the scarring, simply, experience—or disillusionment with the way American men behave when they work together in government, particularly in high-ranking, appointive positions. To some extent I see the way the founder has designed his school as aimed at immunizing, if that can be done, graduates against the diseases bureaucracies seem to plant, and cultivate, in them.

Even in the late 1960s John Adams and his lifelong friend Robert Carswell (d. 1993) understood that such huge organizations as the Department of Defense and IBM simply could not adapt themselves, radically and rapidly, to changed circumstances, to new missions or new technologies. (It is interesting that in the College hymn, "Once to Ev'ry Man and Nation," Adams isolates and extols the line "New occasions teach new duties/Time makes ancient good uncouth.") Specifically, both sensed and understood that such dinosaurs—even then he called IBM a dinosaur—could neither grasp the fact of the coming revolution in processing speed and power nor reconfigure themselves to exploit its gigantic potentials. IBM had the mindset of the American Army of 1935. All was allocated, all sacrificed, to the production of the Main Frame, the huge black elephant that sat, tended by its own fervent keepers, in every office building of every Fortune 500 company in the country. Adams and Carswell saw that semiconductor manufacturing would become a potent source of growth in the American economy: more and more transistors put onto smaller and smaller chips, enabling enormous leaps in productivity... the very big organizations simply didn't have the "temperament"—

that was the right word for it—to master and exploit the opportunity.

American Business (May 1998) writes:

Carswell understood the science behind the change while Adams knew how to organize and motivate people to accomplish the mission. From the people who swept the floors to the sophisticated engineers in antiseptic rooms or obsessed designers working all night on new configurations of microcircuitry and the new manufacturing process, Adams understood the kind of environment and culture that was needed to get people to adapt, to change, to do what was needed. He was able to create an environment in which people felt relaxed and at home with each other even during times of confrontation. This was vital: the work they did at Carswell went home with them. Indeed, they prided themselves on not being able, really, to differentiate between work and play.

Adams had enormous confidence in his work and in the company, confidence of the kind that allowed him to hold onto every share of the company he and Carswell had acquired going public through the frothy, speculative markets of the early and mid-1970s. He always, obsessively, handled financing decisions; he was full of contempt for the myopic, silly schemes of investment bankers and lawyers undertaken for no real reasons other than the generation of fees. Ultimately it was the need for growth, for capital, for a productive association with a more diversified entity, one less at risk from the violent swings of the semiconductor cycle, that brought Adams and Carswell to the decision to sell the company to CPU, the giant maker of microprocessors that formed the brains of the increasingly ubiquitous personal computer.

They closed the transaction (with superb timing) on August 30, 1987. It was finally Adams's genuine respect for the depth and strength of management at CPU as well as his intuitive understanding of the vagaries of the markets that enabled him to continue to hold every new share of CPU he received in 1987 through the panic of October of that year up until the time of his death. This huge investment made up the bulk of his bequest to the foundation that bears his name, and to the college, eventually, that has been the obsession of the last year of his life.

Adams was uninterested in what money could do for him "personally." He had no interest in owning things—property, houses, moveables. He bought nondescript suits from a wholesaler in Los Angeles and rented compact cars from Budget. He ate at nearby Subways or at his desk. He had the green-and-white AMEX card and—according to the *American Business* article—evinced surprise when a friend paid for a meal with a platinum-colored model. What was that? His only indulgences were a 1970 D-Model Steinway concert grand piano and a library of eight thousand books. Yet he had a clinician's interest in the corruptions of money for those susceptible. He remembered, and once cited at a Carswell shareholder's annual meeting, Cotton Mather's *Magnalia Christi Americana* (1702): "Religion hath brought forth Prosperity, and the daughter destroyed the mother... there is a danger lest the enchantments of this world make them forget their errand into the wilderness."

In the months of his dying, John Adams returned to the wilderness he cherished—central Wyoming, at the very edge of the Great Plains. He had domesticated his place in it, as everyone has, but it remained eternally fresh, the source of sustaining dreams, of balm, of (as Parkman remarks) possibility. His disease began foreclosing these possibilities, all but one—making palpable and enduring his notion of how to educate Americans. His final letter, near the end of the book, reaffirms his determination, as he put it, simply to give something back.

Parkman's sense that I might be attracted to service on the board of the new College was unerring, and I write this sentence on the plane, from Denver back to Dulles Airport, having seen our site. We will see what we can make of John Adams's vision.

Josiah Bunting III
Lexington, Virginia
May 1998

CHAPTER I

Setting the Stage

*H*E BELIEVED THAT THE SKY *had a moral function, and that contemplating it induced wonder, a sense of possibility without limit, and inspiration. And he believed that on the High Plains, scoured clean beneath the unbordered canopy of the sky, an American might still dream largely and uncynically. In one of his final notes he left an instruction that the daily curriculum "require and guard zealously a time, of an hour at least, daily, of contemplative solitude. It should be outside for all but the worst months of the year, and the students are to have no books with them when they are alone for such times." He talked often of solitude and silence, and he noted our inability to enjoy even what moments of solitude some accident might have given us, for fear someone might be gaining on us, or that we might drop out of some loop or another. I think he had seen a man standing on the prairie, talking into a cell phone. It was like a French gunboat firing into a continent (where had he read that?), an act, when you stopped to think about it, pitiable and absurd. "We are," he said, "conditioned to feel guilt at being alone."*

He was drawn to the High Plains as his site for another reason. He saw and sensed them as authentic heartland, uncorrected and incorruptible, unthreatened by the whizzing vehicles that hurtled along the transecting ribbons of interstate asphalt, mad to get from Casper to Denver, from Gallup to Amarillo. He loved the endless winds, the vast farms and ranches and their little towns, utterly remote from the manic foolishness of both coasts. They were all, he imagined, still unthreatened by the outlet malls and Wal-Marts, satellite dishes and motel chains; they were all still home to families who had been there four or five generations, and who lived in farmhouses at the center of great squares of alfalfa and wheat, where, at dusk in August, men and women still sat together drinking iced tea. His vision, desperately acute in the last months of his life, and though it had room enough (and was quickened enough by experience) for whiteouts, droughts, and twisters, was yet spun both from love and from hope, and from a conviction that if you taught and raised young people the right way you might still make them better. There remained an innocence in this raw heartland—yes, yes, he would agree, he was a sentimentalist—and it sustained a life that might still preserve the best of that innocence, along with the hardihood it built into a man's character.

The work had to be done in a certain kind of place. It required the right pupils and unusual teachers. You needed to know quite plainly what you wanted the graduates to be, and to have some idea how to take them there, and what the obstacles and the dangers were. They were immense, ridicule was one of them, and Adams was seventy-one, and he was dying.

In a way I am his principal legatee—the man who, almost by happenstance, became the recipient of his notions, some of them hardened to convictions, others more in the nature of directed ruminations; that is, his ideas about the nature of the College toward which he has committed his estate. Its value, almost all of it stock in the company he founded and led for twenty-three years, is a little over $985 million— sufficient to do his bidding in full. Mr. Adams came to me for tax advice seven months ago; now, it seems, I am executive secretary to a board of trustees of a foundation that will translate his wishes into the breathing reality of a new college.

I set before you two of his longer letters of diagnosis and justification. I then present the five chapters (he did not call them that; he resisted the lineaments of finality) in which he tried to order his thoughts on the subject of his College.

On occasion, not often, I will intrude, either with an explanatory comment or, rarely, with the insertion of other Adams letters and my responses to them—always short, comments pertinent to the reader's understanding both of Adams himself and of his ideas about how people should be educated. I ask the reader to remember that this is the work of a man who knew he was not to live for more than a few months; who, equally, would have laughed at my attempt (almost impossible to resist) to make a small drama of the desperate race he must have known himself to be running against the coming of the day when he could no longer work. I once reminded him that that laconic military brute U.S. Grant had had to operate in the same way, fighting to finish his Memoirs even as he was dying of cancer. (Adams encouraged the plainest kind of talk about his illness.) And he said: "Neither laconic nor brutish, and besides, he needed the money."

—Robert Parkman

Here he is:

Dear Robert,

As I told you, I decided several months ago that the material residue of my life and works would be used to establish, build, and sustain an undergraduate college. The papers I am sending you will describe its aims and practices. "Papers" is fair and accurate (the word sounds a little pretentious)—that's really all they are. Several months' worth of musing, a lumpy sequence of several long memoranda and a few letters that together would seem to provide a fair conspectus of what I want done with the money I am leaving the enterprise. It is a serendipity that you, an alumnus of my own university and a tax lawyer, are willing to serve as secretary to our first board: not least because in my present state I can do little more, can offer little more by way of comprehensiveness and precision, than what I now place before you, and a few letters that we may exchange through the ether. The disease is well diffused; my bedside table is a forest of translucent orange vials, like a gathering of silos, but none yielding nourishment, only clumps of hours in which my pain is held at bay.

I am a layman, of course, a businessman, as different by temperament and intellectual endowment from what is called an "academic" as, I suppose, it is possible to be. But I have served on the boards of two universities, of a liberal arts college (which spent most of its time lying to itself, so it would seem, in its pronouncements private and public), and of a boarding school for girls. At our common alma mater (Chicago, 1951) I was soaked in a certain kind of literature that was, implicitly, always about education; and I have never stopped reading—in a way both desultory and voracious—about *how men are educated and how they should be educated.*

(Robert, I am seventy-one. I am too old to write "persons" and to worry over the she and he permutations every time you think I should. Forgive me, will you? "Men" to me is hardy as dust, tragically comprehensive, Thucydidean. Let it be.)

The advice of a great woman is pertinent: "We ought not to sit down and wail, but to be heroic and constructive." I don't know about heroic, but I have had enough of sitting down upon the ground and telling sad stories of the deaths of dreams, of wailing about the state of education we yet call liberal. I'm tired of self-important gibberish about enrollment incentives, deconstruction, tenure, affirmative action, remediation, and all the dreary, weary paraphernalia academic critics and philosophers drag around when they write about what's wrong with so-called higher education. They hide behind their terms like cavalrymen cowering behind dead horses. No; we should do it our way, freshly; building, not wailing. Suppose we could do it the way we wanted to?

Colleges, you know, are not capable of reforming themselves. At least not without the fierce goad of prospective cataclysm or court order. Then they make the changes necessary to save themselves, claiming, however, motives of philosophy. In the ordinary course of business they profess themselves eager for reform, but their professions come to nothing, so hedged are they, so compromised by the requirements for what is called the building of consensus. In truth there is nothing so conservative as a long-serving professor on a committee considering the reform of a curriculum, or almost anything in his university.

His diametric opposite is to be found among one of my long-serving engineers whose life is devoted to *discovering how radical change* can address ancient challenges; his whole prejudice is in favor, in behalf of, useful improvement.

One hundred fifty years ago colleges were brought into being as the progeny of dreams, their purposes idealistic, noble, practical all at once. Study these legacies on the first couple of pages of any of their catalogues. (Robert, I mean the printed artifacts, not what they spray upon their websites or slick up for themselves in the so-called "View Books" they mail out to all who inquire about admission—publications that are a decorator's *Vanity Fair* of PC, stuffed with pictures of posed groups of Sikhs, Caucasians, Native Americans, and so on, seated before Longfellow oaks, gaping gratefully at a nerdy something-or-other in residence....)

This is not digression. There are always, so I say, a couple of pages of mission and history, some of them still lovely and pure. "It was brought into being by the love of liberty." Or "That wisdom might be diffused in a new land, the gift of a bountiful Providence." The missions avow and promise the education of young men, and their preparation for their obligations as virtuous citizens. They still breathe, in the early nineteenth century, the spirit of the seventeenth: "I call therefore a complete and generous education that which fits a man to perform justly, skillfully, magnanimously all the offices, both public and private, of peace and war," in a line we both remember. There are then historical accounts that limn proudly the early struggles of the colleges, the dreams and achievements of the early graduates, not a few mown down in rows at Antietam and Gettysburg. And we find also what a modern university president might today call an integrating vision—an invariable staple of which is that the training of character and the education of intellect may proceed together and can reliably be expected to influence, for good, a graduate's conduct of his life.

So we have that. And then, page three; and page three is about organic chemistry, and page four about endowed chairs, and page five about Title IX, and page six about the new student center. In other words, the mission is still avowed, but avowed only; then forgotten—no longer a pillar, but a decorative pilaster. The only time you hear it is in windy commencement oratory or the nervous opening convocation speech of the new president. What was the Hemingway story, in which the young man prayed to Jesus during the mortar attack on his position, and then, when the firing and shelling had moved farther up the line, forgot about Jesus, and never thought of Him again? Do you think the newly hired assistant professor of economics cares anything about virtue, or the obligations to their country of liberally educated graduates?

So the catalogues promise one thing (usually something to do with virtuous citizenship or the efficacy of liberal education), but their promise has no more meaning for a new undergraduate in this last decade of the worst century yet than a back issue of the *Kenyon Review*.

In their frail beginnings these colleges were the progeny of bright dreams, a radiating faith, and practical needs—all three. Virtually all were founded by the several religious denominations, not necessarily as sectarian institutions but committed to the teaching of religious texts—the Bible—and in significant measure to the preparation of some graduates for the Christian ministry. Chapel was the heart of daily communitarian life: here the president of the college, ordinarily a D.D., preached moral texts from the Old and New Testaments—finding inexhaustible lessons in them, lessons to serve the lives of ordinary men. Christian Apologetics meant informed explanation of parables and mysteries, not Apologies for allowing revealed religion a role in undergraduate education.

Nowadays neither the Cross (nor the Star of David) nor the Flag has anything but the thinnest, most begrudged presence on the campuses of universities esteemed as the brightest citadels of academic excellence. "Chapel" is but the remembered morning ritual of a jettisoned past (though yet cherished in the memory by men older than I who "sat through"—great phrase!—hundreds of them, in Hanover, New Hampshire, or Davidson, North Carolina, as the country foundered in depression or armed itself for the war against Hitler and Japan). No, chapel is vanished tone and tint—as indeed is any enforced allegiance to moral behavior of the kind enjoined in the Books common to the great faiths of our country. And in their care to avoid the merest chance of giving offense to any, by taking stout-hearted positions on such moral issues, universities nowadays unite to an essential soullessness, a cowardice they are pleased to call "Regard for All Positions." Indeed, any controversy so engendered is at once forced into the ritualistic genuflection before a new God: The God of Consensus, Himself the child of an even greater secular Divinity—*Consensus-Building*. Thus are our children to be educated liberally.

Yet for me our collective history demonstrates most plainly that the aims of the founders of these colleges, exactly right for their time, remain perfectly apt for our own. "The troubles of our proud and angry dust are from eternity, and shall not fail." The business of undergraduate education remains the cultivation of character and mind, of instinct and ability of leadership and service. It is the way that men should live and behave in our culture and our country that is the proper business of our colleges. I don't mean as ministers and architects, chemists and executives; I mean as citizens. I set the education of character and virtue at least as high among our obligations as the preparation of intellect for a lifetime of self-education.

When we talked, you bristled amiably at my phrase "virtuous and disinterested service." Our College would consecrate itself to preparing its graduates for lives of public service of one kind or another, emphatically including politics, as well as work in government in all its usages and forms, in voluntary service to community, in uniform, in teaching in our public schools.

My adjectives are of an eighteenth-century utility if not coinage, and they mean exactly what you, as an educated man, must take them to mean. *Virtuous:* doing what is right, in accordance with the searching and pitiless dictates of conscience. *Disinterested:* motivated only by the notion of doing for our enterprise what it needs, not what I need. You will no doubt remember Jefferson's handsome encomium to Washington: "His integrity was most pure, his justice the most inflexible I have ever known; no motives of interest or consanguinity, of friendship or hatred, being able to bias his decision." That is what I mean by disinterested.

For I look out upon a culture and politics that is now but a scabrous vision, in another phrase you will remember—a vision to dizzy and appall: the rankest unseemliness in government in all its usages, reeking money, ill-temper, indulged ambition, self-absorption, desperate confusion as to means and ends both, meanspiritedness, adultery, an unwillingness to risk greatly. Can it not be that men and women of parts humane, courageous, disinterested, and cultivated can be brought to serve the country and commonweal?

Whom shall we send, and who will go for us? That is, how will we decide on those who should be invited to join our enterprise? Who will teach them? What and how can we teach them—that is, teach them in ways that promise to influence conduct for good, rather than simply populating their memories and minds with quiddities and anecdotes that a decade will exterminate, or teaching them some sort of trade.

As for our site—I have found it and will tell you about it later. It is far, far from Washington and New York, and almost as far from Los Angeles.

Time was when an A.B. like yours or mine, from the University of Chicago or, say, Columbia, was a testimonial both noble and accurate to something beyond a four-year residence and a set of examinations safely negotiated. Perhaps in these places it still is. This quiet credential for our graduates must proclaim that the bearer is an American citizen of integrity, of an avid and cultivated patriotism, of intellectual self-reliance, of a willingness to earn and re-earn wisdom, indifferent to the blandishments of celebrity and money and things. We know each other so little that all this must still sound to you like the idle velleities of an old and dying and rich man. I assure you, my dear Robert, I am in dead earnest. The things our country requires are simply not the things our colleges are prepared to deliver. So let us have our shot. Think, in the meantime, about this: our first graduates might leave the College around 2005. They may expect to live until a day within twenty or thirty years of the twenty-second century. How is what they will need to live their lives in accordance with our mission for them—and how is this to differ from what we might have done for another generation two hundred or a hundred years ago?

I am on the painkiller Percoset and need two more. You're free for now.

Believe me to be, your grateful friend,
John Adams

MY DEAR ROBERT,

As I look out at my country, look out at it as an invalid from a broad window in my house in Wyoming, a window that faces directly east, I see and hear and watch and read and understand a terrible reality, and it fills me with both a horror and a sadness that themselves defy articulation. Mine is a secular shadow of Cardinal Newman's distress a century and a half ago. Newman, in his watching of the life of his church and his culture, could make out only "the tokens so faint and broken, of a superintending design... and the prevalence and intensity of sin, the pervading idolatries, the corruptions, the dreary hopeless irreligion, that condition of the whole race, so fearfully yet exactly described in the Apostle's words, 'having no hope and without God in the world.'"

I see such tokens so faint and broken of the designs of America's Founders. The design was the projection of a new nation, a City upon a Hill to which all pledged their sacred honor. But the new nation conceived in liberty is now mostly a melancholy chaos of dispirit, selfishness, self-regard, and calculation—a cacophony of suspicion and rage. A vision, like Newman's aching diagnosis of his culture, to dizzy and appall.

My enterprise, tiny in the vast scale of institutions established to educate our citizenry, is no dream of human perfectibility, no effort at creating standardized human entities who will "behave" in a certain manner, who will enroll behind the banners of certain expected professions, whose politics will be those of Aristotle and Burke or of Locke and J.S. Mill. We will aim to educate a fewscore young persons to be virtuous and disinterested citizens and leaders; patriots who more than self their country love; citizens who when they are not virtuous in their lives and works will know they are not and will labor always to sustain their determination to be virtuous, self-mastering, drawn to the accumulation of a moderate sufficient property only, and educated liberally but avid in their commitment always to remain liberally self-educating.

I have accumulated a great fortune, but I can fairly write that the fortune was not the intention. There is a text, illuminating and memorable, that is usefully if not wholly appropriate. It is in the Book of Kings in the Old Testament, Chapter 3, verses 6–14. The Lord has asked Solomon what he would hope to have, as king. The Lord, delighted in Solomon's response, gives him those good things for which he has not asked: they are the unexpected, unsought concomitants of a life nobly consecrated to doing right.

I am made glad at the prospect that virtually my entire fortune is to be devoted to this work. By the simplest of calculations, the income assured by its proper and prudent management will sustain the College, as I conceive its needs and size, forever, in all respects. No child need pay a penny to enroll, study, and be graduated; and no building, no maintenance expense, no emolument for any who live and teach and lead upon its demesne need be drawn from any fund other than that which I shall leave in my will.

You know that I am sick. The phrase "this kind of cancer" rolls easily off the tongues of those who treat me, the "my doctors" of whom you've heard me talk. This kind of cancer and its untrammelled metastases, the reconnaissance patrols and colonizing combat teams it sends forth with rich stocks of ammunition and supplies, should declare their final victories sometime during the next nine or ten months. "Even when it gets fully into your bones," one of the flossy young oncologists assured me, "we can now deal with it"; by which he means we can deal with the pain to which you will be subjected. They have a thing, he's showed me it, that you can squeeze in your hand, that releases an analgesic, a morphine derivative, that will give relief. Meantime I will write you and will send you directions of a general character that will provide at least the guidance of a summary for those who will bring my small and final dream into being.

With high esteem and appreciation.

Yours,
John Adams

Note: Mr. Adams employs an array of verbs and phrases of volition: "I would hope," "I hope that," "I think that," "I will propose," "I urge," "I suggest," and so on. But the trustees charged with the establishment of the College, with the early translation of inspiration and concept into practical reality, have understood them to denote absolute intention or considered and settled conviction. The donor used verb phrases interchangeably, softening their impact—this was absolutely characteristic of the way he dealt with people—not out of diffidence but from a desire to take his colleagues or friends or subordinates, so to speak, into his confidence. In the time I knew him I learned that "I would hope that" meant "I want." He imagined the lawyers would call some of his wishes "precatory" (that is, I hope you'll do this if you can); but, though there are two lawyers among us—the five trustees of the foundation he established, to which his funds and his estate will soon have been fully committed—we have not taken his wishes in this way. We will work to do what we believe Mr. Adams wanted done.

There is also a question of his last illness and its possible effect on the clarity of his thought, and on the means available to him of communi-

cating fervor or relative (for him) indifference, adamant demand or sim-
ple wish. It is always appealing for heirs to remember the decedent as
lucid to the last—"His mind was sharp as a razor." But Adams truly
was lucid to the last. Late on the morning of the day before he died,
lying on his back and looking up at the screen on which he could write
or send and receive his e-mails, he gave specific instructions to trustees on
the matter of including the Russian romantics in one of the music courses
he insisted the curriculum contain. He wrote, the keyboard askew at
his hips, "All the Opus 23 Preludes of Rachmaninoff, even the bad
ones—and use the Ashkenazi disc for the G-Minor. Also I want
Kalennikov and Glazunov, with G, not The Seasons *but the Violin*
Concerto." He relished the thought of how such music would sound to
the students, who would hear it for the first time on the demesne, in the
Laramie Mountains in Wyoming, where, he fantasized, it would become
as natural to their ears as the endless winds and the music they had
heard all their lives before they came to the College.

—R.P.

CHAPTER 2

What Is Our Mission?

I MAY STATE IT SIMPLY. The College's mission is the preparation of virtuous and disinterested citizens and leaders for the Republic.

There is a law of human enterprise that would seem to insist that the simplest things are also those most difficult to do well. The achievement of an aim like ours demands a careful examination of the issues it presents. To frame the question another way, what kind of a college might most usefully serve such a mission? How? Let us for a while assume general agreement as to terms and their meanings: "virtuous," "disinterested," "citizens," "leaders"—all words to which we will have to return presently. We must answer five questions:

1. What is our mission?
2. Who should our students be?
3. How should they live?
4. What should they learn?
5. Who should lead—and teach—them?

The first question we answered above. As for the second, my own ideas are so different from those now employed by our famous universities that I hesitate—almost—to place them before you. Suffice it to say that I do not think such places understand how to judge the potential, in young persons, for growing wise. They make their judgments on "scores" that demonstrate only the ability to achieve success at attaining such "scores." The push-up, I am told, qualifies one for efficiency at performing... push-ups.

I will next propose the circumstances of their lives, when they are in residence on the College demesne: how they shall be asked to live in the community of the College, and how, in the way they live, they may be so circumstanced as to *learn*.

Is there some body of information, some corpus of knowledge or of accumulated wisdom, that our students—given our mission—should learn and comprehend? Should we not also insist that the predisposition to learn, ceaselessly and passionately, be planted in them as undergraduates—that they develop the proverbial love of learning to which all university presidents and commencement orators pledge themselves, but which few citizens sustain? And must they not also, simply, learn how to think, how to analyze issues carefully and patiently, their minds unbeclouded by the grey film of emotion or unexamined premise? To such large questions we must devote a part of our work. And we must also labor to develop in our students the skills needed by citizens who are to live in our democratic Republic, the skills and indeed the habits of useful service to the state.

It is amusing that, when our countrymen idly grope for exemplars of brilliant intellection, they invariably mention brain surgeons and rocket scientists, neither category of which, so far as I can see, has any necessary connection to the kind of mind and character necessary to useful citizenship or to the arts of leading. Indeed it might be urged that such laboriously cultivated skills (with certain uses in the world no doubt) are antipathetic to the kinds of wisdom that citizenship and leading demand. But this is another wood to thresh, and a later one.

What will we ask our students to learn? How will they live while they are students at the College? Learning implies knowledge; knowledge implies nothing to our purpose unless we act on it in some way. That is, the fact that we know something or think something does not mean we will usefully employ, to some purpose, what we know. It is in the circumstances of our lives, what we are, how we live, what we "do," that we translate knowledge into action, into the way we choose to live and to serve in communities, and in the way we make our lives in the world. It is in the reciprocal action of learning and living, particularly among the young who are living together, that the knowledge they are gaining may be acted upon, may be converted into something I call mother wit (a term that has quite gone out of fashion), perhaps even wisdom, perhaps even the regular habit of good action. We remember the word "virtuous" in our mission: "natural reason... retains the power to know good from evil, and to discern truth and falsehood. But it is powerless to do what it knows to be good," as Thomas à Kempis says in *The Imitation of Christ.* Colleges and countries prattle pathetically about "lessons learned," as though learning a lesson will lead ineluctably to its appropriate employment. Against the unremitting and rapacious insistences of Ego, Will, and Desire, however, lessons learned are neither bulwarks nor beacons; they are intellectual *divertissements* at worst, promptings and instructions to conscience at best.

How therefore should we establish our community of pupils and teachers? How should it be organized? Where should it be, and how large? Again, all these questions must be answered with particular solicitude for how our students may learn things, may develop habits of living that will be useful in their lives as virtuous and disinterested citizens of the United States.

Presently, we will consider the question of size. As to the character of the College's form of education, we are joining an ancient debate, namely, whether we may presume to make men wiser and also, in some sense, *better.* I am without illusion. John Adams described the dilemma to Thomas Jefferson in a letter dated December 1819:

Have you ever found one single example of a nation thoroughly corrupted that was afterwards restored to virtue?... Will you tell me how to prevent riches from becoming the effects of temperance and industry? Will you tell me how to prevent luxury from producing effeminacy?

Yet all these ought not to discourage us from exertion, for... I believe no effort in favor of virtue is lost, and all good men ought to struggle, both by their counsel and their example.

What should they learn, and how should they live? I know that, twenty years from now, or fifty, those who will be graduates of our College may heed the counsels of ambition before answering the demands of honor and conscience; that they may bear false witness in order to advance themselves in politics or business; may be temerarious in action or counsel; self-deluding, self-righteous, avid for material gain and ill-content with what Aristotle called a moderate and sufficient property. I know that the bruising traumas of moral life may leave them desolated or undone, may predispose them to dark cynicism or lazy *complaisance*. Our aims for the College are certainly noble ones, but my expectations cannot be unrealistic. So that those things that we need to do, in order to combat the ungovernable demands of passion, or ambition and will, of the peculiar American frenzy to establish invidious material distinction over our neighbor, will require that we *train* our students at the same time as we are educating them, or aiding them to educate themselves. The two words seem antipathetic, but they need not be. To habituate our students to certain ways of living, to ways of "conducting themselves," is an urgent imperative—and this is training. To nourish and cultivate their brains, to make them prudently skeptical, imaginative, reasonable thinkers, likely to sustain through their lives the capacity for wonder, for the joy of hearing strange melodies or seeing dappled things, for the hearing of inspirations and intuitions that come unbidden and to make them capable of long periods of sustained thinking—this is education. If our graduates are to become the effective citizens and leaders we will work to prepare, our College must work at both things at once.

Beyond all argument a small college will answer our need best: a small college with what, I hardly need say, will be an unusual and distinct *ethos* and culture. Famous universities that trumpet their size as a means of demonstrating their... what? but they know not what, exactly... deploy gargantuan resources (in the getting of which they have often been faithless to their collective consciences, if they have any) to sustain armies of scholars, ant-like, at their researches, and dozens of postgraduate divisions and faculties to train up and credential fresh recruits for the professions. But such institutions are but agglomerations of people and facilities working in the same cities and upon the same campuses, screaming their rage or bellowing their delight at the same athletic games, busy in undertakings that have little to do with each other. A postgraduate student, preoccupied with his own research (i.e., looking things up), listlessly directs traffic in an undergraduate seminar on contemporary fiction, then returns to his carrel or work station across town. His contribution to the work enjoined by our mission would be zero—indeed, perhaps less than zero.

Our students must be led. They must be taught. Who should lead and teach them? Certainly, persons whose lives in some useful sense they share and influence, persons drawn to such work because they love teaching the young and delight in watching their progress and in contributing to it. In a small college, one in which virtually all know or are known to each other, pupils and teachers alike, in which all are engaged in a common mission, all full of heart and allegiance to our *ethos*—here, the real, stick-to-the-ribs work of an education to our purpose may thrive. Again, in working to answer the question—How should they live?—it seems reasonable that they live among a representation of their American contemporaries that is, in fact, truly representative. Later we will look carefully at how to build, and how to replenish, annually, our studentry. It must be national in character, but the criteria I have in mind for making our selections are, as I say, quite different from those colleges that we call and that, without embarrassment, call themselves elite.

I use the term "small college." And yet I want ours to be big enough to provide our community a dense plenitude of individual difference and of many kinds of talent—a vital concourse in fact of hundreds of sharply individuated characters, a plenitude of true as opposed to fustian eccentricity. While a radiating purposiveness will inflect the whole of our enterprise, that purposiveness will not mean that those who will join us will be worn to a common quality by it—except in the quality of their virtue and character. But an avowed staple of our *ethos* will be a consciousness, zealously sustained and determined, of the cardinal importance of unfettered individual conscience and expression, the latter never fettered in its willingness to speak up in behalf of opinion or conviction however unusual or heterodox. The smothering preemptive miasma of opinion that, singularly grotesque in its presumption, delights to call itself "liberal" will never descend upon our College.

(The accompaniment of this condition is often the speech code, a common cataloguing of words, phrases, spoken ideas, and opinions that, to the minds of the authors of the codes, may be offensive to members or categories of members of universities. The near neighbor of the speech code is the categorical euphemism, a means of expression by which the fearful utterer is able to communicate the essence of his thought without giving offense to its recipient. Arguments in behalf of such lunacies masquerade as solicitude for what men call their feelings; truth, however, has no feeling, though it is the largest casualty of the codemaker's solicitude.)

The young delight in their membership in singular, distinct, communities: those for example of high schools for the scientifically gifted, or of certain military regiments, ships' companies, teams of athletes. Their attachments to those things Burke called the little platoons are given without calculation or reservation—most particularly to those human enterprises that demand the most of them. "Do not think the Jesuit discipline hard," Cardinal Newman wrote a new Catholic soon to enter the priesthood. "It will bring you to Heaven." I am certain that our College may be so contrived as to endow its graduates with the "heritage of honor and self-sacrifice" that the grateful graduate of another American college—George Marshall—at the beginning of the present century saw as its most precious gift to him.

Our enterprise will require that we enroll but a small number of students (I have in mind about 1,200 in residence at any one time), and that all of them be undergraduates. I imagine they will quickly identify themselves—and be so identified—as an elite, and this delights me. The Latin root of elite is *to elect:* in our circumstance, we are to enroll those we elect out of confidence in their aptness for our purpose; and those who enroll will have elected our way of education because they believe in its mission. ("Elite" is now promiscuously applied to any group of men and women assembled for some purpose, which has attained the raiment of *cachet*. Thus, "She has joined the elite circle of high-fashion models always sought by the leading couturiers," and such.)

We will insist from the beginning on an ardent ethic of benevolence and magnanimity in the relations of our pupils, among themselves, their mentors, and their professors—indeed among all members of our community. By this I mean chiefly that intellectual discourse, however passionate, should be as forbearing as it is ardent, as in easy conversation among dear friends. My own colleagues tell me that academic life is eaten out by spite and rancor, vindictiveness and selfish calculation, just as contemporary politics feeds, when not battening upon money, upon the venomous nourishments of vindictiveness. That may be. The inference is that since most colleges feature such behavior, and since many of our graduates will undertake lives of public service and politics, they had better arm themselves for the bruising viciousness of both worlds, the latter particularly.

But such counsel is contemptible on two grounds. First, we should not prepare students by compromising principles and standards we know to be right in order that they may more reliably advance themselves later on when they enter upon their professions. Second, because we have seen the chastening power of example. Those in public positions who are vilified and savaged, and who make no response but continue to do their duty calmly and quietly, build for themselves over many years reputations that are not only unassailable but that are finally the very causes of their achievements in our country's behalf. I think at once of the triumvirate of Washington, Lincoln, and George

Marshall. It was their reputations for disinterestedness, for self-mastery, that always made their counsels so valuable, and assured that they would be heard, as the honest advice of men loyal to country and truth before party and self. (As Cicero said, "For to suppose that any permanent reputation can be won by pretense, or empty display, or hypocritical talk, or by putting on an insincere facial expression, would be a serious misapprehension. A genuine, glorious reputation strikes deep roots and has wide ramifications.")

Nor can I myself omit to observe that a hardening orthodoxy of fashionable opinion (the fashionable having been darkly transmuted to what is now called *politically correct* opinion) is the singular enemy of any enterprise that presumes to call itself either intellectual or academic. We venerate men of mind like George Orwell and Edmund Burke (we might indeed in our bereavement adduce the luminous name of Isaiah Berlin) precisely because they gave eloquent voice, always confident, always unafraid, to ideas and opinions unstraitened by the cloying orthodoxies of the day, or uninfluenced by their calculations of how an audience that would comprise enemies as well as friends was likely to receive them. "There can be no philosophy where fear of consequences is greater than love of truth," said John Stuart Mill.

Now I wish to define—for the purposes of our College—the four words about whose meaning I asked your patience earlier. I take them in reverse order:

Leaders

I have in mind a college that will prepare Americans for positions of authority and responsibility in the various public professions. I do not exclude, certainly, those of commerce and technology, those of private business. But I have in mind particularly an enterprise that will fit them for appointed or elective offices in governments; that will so infect their consciences with a passion for the public good, that they will serve, and come to lead, in the various volunteer works—service to communities, schools, churches, hospitals, universities—that are the sustaining human fuel of such activities. I have in mind an education, too, that will particularly suit them for professional lives made in teaching (especially in the primary and secondary schools, as opposed to universities), in the ministries of the various faiths, in the armed services, and the like of these. I do not mean to conflate military service with religious—except in the sense that each ideally "calls" men and women actuated less by a desire for ascendancy and authority than by a compulsion to give and to serve, and to give, as Loyola said, without counting the cost.

Remembering that those we will enroll will be very young (I propose that we admit those who have completed their third, rather than fourth, year of high school), and that therefore we cannot in full confidence predict what they will be "like" at thirty or fifty, I keep in mind two categories of leaders in particular.

The first comprises those on whom history, or circumstance, simply flings a mantle, as it does in its jaggedly unpredictable ways: sometimes on individuals, sometimes on generations, sometimes on countries. A great historian at midcentury wrote a life of Catherine of Aragon, saying that one of the things that attracted him especially to her sad, sad life was "the way persons by no means gifted with genius but strategically placed" may influence the course of events. That is to say, the opportunities or necessities of leading, whether church vestries or universities, cabinets or companies, seem to devolve, and often, upon people who have not sought them actively, who did not feel themselves marching with destiny or fulfilling boyish dreams or attaining the culminating points of careers. No. Someone died. Or a bored committee, tired of politics, said, Jones, get him. Or a brilliant but diffident young woman who has made a reputation as an editor is plucked suddenly from her quiet niche and elevated to the presidency of a publishing house. It happens all the time. For every Lincoln (whose ambition Herndon said was an engine that never stopped) there is a Truman; for every Eisenhower, a Bradley. Those prospective leaders who do not recognize in themselves any significant desire to lead, or even an unusual capability to lead, are often themselves admired for qualities of character that observers sense will *make* them strong leaders. And often they do. Let us have the satisfaction, many years hence, that our graduates, so circumstanced, are ready to discharge the responsibilities they will not have sought.

I am thinking also of prospective leaders who have always wanted to lead, whose ambitions drive them quite consciously to covet positions of leadership, places and mantles of power, authority, and fame. It is this category, if we may call it that, which will furnish us a large share of our students—that is, candidates who even in adolescence will recognize their opportunity and sense in it a means to ready themselves for lives of responsibility and a certain kind of distinction. The way our students will be required to live during their residence will be of largest benefit to *them.* Conduct that is selfless and often self-effacing, enjoined by a regimen peculiar to the College's culture, is to be required of all, as we will see. Its greatest benefit in my view is reserved for the young, confidently ambitious matriculants to the College.

James Madison insisted on a "republican remedy for the diseases most incident to republican government." He understood that much of the remedy must lie in the "character of persons holding office in the... national government." They must be liberally educated, and bound to remain liberally self-educating for the rest of their lives. They must be versatile in their interests and aptitudes. They must be "cosmopolitan and virtuous, and capable of disinterested judgment"—that is, of judgments taken with deliberate solicitude for the welfare of the group only, and not of oneself. Again and again we will return to the question of character, the character of leaders and citizens both. Working to influence character for good will be a constant and principal obligation of the College. It will be work no doubt much criticized. It will be terribly out of joint with contemporary ideas about "the purposes of education." Yet this effort to train and influence character is more important than anything we do to *educate* students' intellects. Not less important, not equally important, *more* important. An ordinary citizen of sound mind and sterling character is infinitely better—as a product of our College, as a future leader—than a brilliant and cultivated intellectual of "flexible" character.

Leadership unites integrity and resolution. A good example is in Darwin's *Autobiography,* where he records his admiration for his Uncle Josiah Wedgwood, who was "silent and reserved... the very type of an upright man, with the clearest judgment. I do not believe any power on earth could have made him swerve an inch from what he considered the right course."

There is a statement imputed, I think, to Aldous Huxley, to the effect that the purpose of education is to make men know what they ought to do, and then do it, whether they want to or not. In educating (and training) "for character," we are serving Mr. Huxley's purpose.

"Leadership," as the word is nowadays flung about (every airport bookstore in our country puffs paperbacks promising *Eight Keys to Successful Leadership*), has little connection to this. Leadership is now understood as something that will confer authority, cachet, and the appurtenances of money: something that will lead us to glittering stages on which we may make a brave (and surely visible) bustle of exercising power. The notion of stages is particularly important, for stages imply both scripts and audiences. Leadership so conceived fastens on two dispositions both familiar in Shakespeare (many of whose plays, incidentally, will be read, whole, by our students):

> Then, since this earth affords no joy to me
> But to command, to check, to o'erbear such
> As are of better person than myself,
> I'll make my heaven to dream upon the crown,
> And whiles I live, t'account this world but
>   hell....
> > *Henry VI, Part III,* Act III, Scene ii

> ...But 'tis a common proof,
> That lowliness is young ambition's ladder,
> Whereto the climber-upward turns his face;
> But when he once attains the upmost round,
> He then unto the ladder turns his back,
> Looks in the clouds, scorning the base degrees
> By which he did ascend.
> > *Julius Caesar,* II, i

Who does not know such men, such leaders, in his own life? The latter, particularly, for whom the earned accolade of a soft green fairway next to a ghastly pink domicile, in a place a thousand miles from the frame house of his birth, has become the lived expression of the American dream—the dream bounded, however, by an invisible fence for the dogs, a visible fence for common humanity, and a detachment of uniformed dunderheads, lawnboys, and urologists, all retained to assure such masters of the universe, American Tories, practitioners of "leadership," no longer need see, much less remember, the base degrees by which they did ascend.

The College will stand out for a different idea about leading: the idea of unhesitating willingness to embrace responsibility without calculation of reward or risk—or reward, in any case, of the kind that success at "leadership" promises. Its conviction about leading is lodged in the notion of community and country before self, and in that of steady long allegiance to principled responsibility. For example, consider the allegiance of that generation of military and naval officers who remained with the colors from 1918 to 1941, disregarded, ill-paid, unpromoted—allegiant to a cause only because it was right. But prepared to serve for that reason alone. Such kinds of leading cannot be "taught," in any conventional way, but they can be learned. One way by which we propose to help such learning is a means common in our country two centuries ago, but now as distant, as quaint to the sense as a Shaker chair, but just as functional: *Emulation.*

For honor travels in a strait so narrow,
Where one but goes abreast. Keep then the path,

For emulation hath a thousand sons
That one by one pursue.
                Troilus and Cressida, III, iii

Citizens

Some years ago there was a movie adaption of James Michener's small novel of the Korean War, *The Bridges at Toko-Ri.* One remembers from it an old admiral, how his face registered the news that his protégé and young friend, a pilot, had been killed on a mission over North Korea. His plane, we had seen, had been brought down, crash-landing on a cold, brown hillock near the coast. He had tried to defend himself with a service revolver, but had been surrounded, wounded, and killed. His death was squalid and most pitiable. He had died brave and terrified, and almost alone.

The pilot had been a tribune of that American generation that had reached its majority around the time of Pearl Harbor. He had served for four years in the Second World War, gone to law school, married, had two little girls, and begun a practice in Denver. He had kept his reserve commission in the Marines. This was why he was killed, ten thousand miles from home, in a strange war whose purposes he perhaps did not fully understand, but in his service to which he gave without cavil fifty summers, fifty Christmases, his lovely bride, his daughters, his work, ten thousand sunsets, his life. The admiral mused—it is almost the last thing in the movie—*Where do we get such men as these?*

(One cannot forbear adding a bleakly bland formulation of Trotsky's: You may not be interested in war, but war is interested in you.)

War had found the young officer. And at one level the answer to the admiral's query is curt and simple. We get such young men through the draft or on reserve assignment. They join us and do what they are told. Not a few are killed. It is the cost of doing business if you are a powerful democracy in the twentieth and twenty-first centuries. Surely in our national future crouch hundreds of wars, waiting silently for men, and now—barbarous to think—for women to join them. We are, said Richard Eberhart, no farther advanced than in our ancient furies. For every Shiloh and Saratoga, there will be a dozen Khe Sanhs and Kuwaits. Our students should be ready for them.

Our graduates will compose but the tiniest cohort of Madison's republican remedy, and yet for this reason their training and education at the College must be most carefully wrought in order to achieve our ends—"republican" in the sense of virtuous; virtuous in the sense of selfless and dutiful; simple in personal wants; scrupulous and honorable in discharging all commitments however paltry; devoted to country. Whether they are one day to be mayors of towns in New York or Nebraska or to dispute a barricade in Asia, we must prepare and educate them to their obligations as American citizens, not least—I quote Pericles writing of Athens—by leading them to fall in love with their country. And by living that love for their country in the unhesitating provision of services to its needs, when such provision is recognized, required, or sought.

We are now a nation of two hundred sixty million, untold millions of whom are utterly alienated from the benefits and obligations of citizenship, bent only on building high fences so that none may see them when they sink, too exhausted to do anything but look at games on television, after the day's work.

Ephraim Wood, shoemaker and farmer in late eighteenth-century Concord, Massachusetts, served his town for several years as selectman and clerk, carrying out his duties during the first days of the American Revolution. When he died in 1814, he was eulogized thus:

> In him were united those qualities and virtues, which formed a character at once amiable, useful, respectable, and religious. Early in life he engaged in civil and public business, and by a judicious and faithful discharge of duty acquired confidence and reputation with his fellow citizens and the public.... [T]he rights and liberties of his country were near his heart, and he was a warm and zealous defender of those against all encroachments.... In domestic life his disposition and example were highly amiable and worthy. As a Christian, he was devout and humble, sincere and ardent. Having lived the life, he died the death of the righteous. He was a true disciple of Washington, a friend to "liberty with order."

Will it be possible to get such men and such women as these in the year 2000? Is any citizen nowadays a true disciple of anyone, save madmen who set up religious communes or command private armies of the dispossessed?

The stuff of human character is unchanging. I do not doubt that. Nor do I doubt that character and citizenship can be formed by the family, faith, education, training, or habit. Such things are chiefly but not wholly molded before we become young adults, and mainly by the influences of the larger culture in which we grow up; today, that larger culture is inescapably unhelpful.

Disinterested

Thomas Jefferson said that John Adams was "as disinterested as the Being who made him." A burden of our mission must be the development of this disinterestedness in our pupils.

We mean the word in two senses. Each implies a deliberate scouring away of egoistic ambition or calculation. When Matthew Arnold in his famous formulation exhorts us to learn and propagate the best that has been said and thought in the world, he enjoins our spirit of disinterestedness: we must school ourselves to see things as they really are, vigilantly correcting for the urgings of our own biases or prejudices, whatever their origins. By common assent of educated and disinterested judges, certain classics of literature are appropriately exalted, criticized, admired, or understood by succeeding generations. In our understanding of *their* excellence, we form the habit of judging with disinterest other artifacts of human achievement. We work at becoming "objective."

The quality of being disinterested is directly linked to my purpose for the College: building as a habit of conduct the mastery of all urgings that would drive a man from his duty and the elimination of all calculations of benefit or gain. It is close to what General Douglas MacArthur once called "Patriotic Self-abnegation."

This is to say that the College must work to make unself-regarding conduct a habit. No one felicitated Robert E. Lee or Patrick Henry on his moral courage. Each simply did what he thought he ought to do, regardless of the consequences, without any thought of personal gain. Provision for one exception is made, most beautifully expressed in Lee's farewell to the Army of Northern Virginia: "the satisfaction that proceeds from consciousness of duty faithfully performed."

Perhaps needless to say, our model is not some juiceless monster of perfection, a being without compassion, without moral imagination. Self-reliance of conduct does not mean isolation or self-absorption. It means acting after taking final counsel with oneself, acting comfortably and abiding the consequences knowing that one has discharged one's duty. The doing is resolute because resolution has become habitual. It is a classical ideal.

I know that Americans, when they hear the word "classical," think of horrid and dutiful immersions in boring wastes of old music or incomprehensible texts that have no relevance to their own lives. It is as though, when they receive their degrees, they offer a prayer of thanks that, thank God, that's over. I would expect the graduate from our College to be reading a commentary on the *Iliad* on the way to his first job interview. If you think that is an unattainable ideal, I would point you to the public school–educated subalterns in the British Army in the First World War who behaved just so on their way to the trenches.

I believe that by having students live at very close quarters, and in a certain way, in a community in which the actions of all somehow touch the lives and interests of all others, we can habituate our young men and women to living disinterested (if not wholly unself-regarding) lives. Every tendency of our age is toward the opposite *ethos,* one in which all actions are taken only with particular reference to how they will advance the individual, to assure for him the tinsel accolade of celebrity, whose useful recompense is approximately that of a piece of chocolate or a cigarette; or to gain him authority, money, or, if he is close to coming unhinged, the ignoble satisfactions of seeing his name placed upon buildings, stadia, interstate access roads, and the like of that. Our student, contrariwise, must find that his duty yields him the satisfactions not of power or invidious distinction, nor of exalted status or money, but only of knowing that he has done his best by and for those who have depended on him, and that he may have done that best, and often, when he did not want to, when he was exhausted, or when he doubted the wisdom of the duty prescribed for him, or when a hundred other obligations competed for his attention.

The inculcation of the habit of disinterested conduct will be difficult. Its results will be neither knowable nor provable for many years. A half-century from now, when our earliest graduates may, like Cincinnatus, yearn only for a time of quiet husbandry (or what may pass for its equivalent in 2050), a watchful friend may assess the character of his life and its contribution. Perhaps he may fairly call it "disinterested." Even then, however, we shall not know whether it was our College that "made" him that way, or the circumstances of his growth from the cradle, his Sunday school, his teachers, his hardscrabble life on the western prairie—or a lonely impulse that commended him to us, and made him thrive and grow in our community.

Virtuous

In his essay *Of Education* (1644), Milton sets himself the task of preparing "the right path of a virtuous and noble education," that is, an education that would inculcate standards of private morality and adherence to them, and, at the same time, fit its scholars for active lives of service to profession and country. The teachers in his ideal institution would lead their pupils—by force of character and example—to the "study of learning and the admiration of virtue," stirring them up with "high hopes of living to be brave men and worthy patriots, dear to God and famous to all ages."

Virtue, as our College must champion it and as John Adams described it—*republican virtue*—is a positive passion for the public good. It must be a passion strong enough to overcome what Jefferson saw as "the sole antagonist of virtue, self-love... [that] leads us constantly by our propensities to self-gratification in violation of our moral duties to others."

To read these bestowals of the luminous minds of the seventeenth and eighteenth centuries at the turn of the twenty-first is to set down in bereavement our understanding of their distance from us. And we must acknowledge a corollary even more lacerating: that all citizens of good sense acknowledge the truth of the observation—and that their acknowledgment begins and ends in a shrug. They accept the condition as truth ineluctable, as though the self-regard and corruption which are the chief features of the way we conduct the polity's business today are beyond amendment, and their practitioners beyond chastisement. We acknowledge, implicitly, that only those who know how to manipulate the system may advance themselves, or be advanced by the polity, to positions of authority.

"Virtuous" for the College must mean a way of living that both exalts and works to inculcate qualities of character that are required by those who—whether in government or not—will be public persons: not only the classical virtues of Courage, Temperance, Wisdom, and Justice, but also those that are among the chief virtues of the faiths of our Fathers—Charity and Faith, which, Aquinas believed, are complementary to the classical virtues. To live in frugal circumstances, to consider how we may shoulder our brother's burden before we lift our own, to work in unself-advertising solitude for a long time, to accomplish a task that we have been given, always to tell the exact truth, and to tell it fearlessly whatever the circumstance—such are the modes and habits of composing noble lives (when was the last time you heard an American use the world "noble" in cold blood?) that will be among the College's practices.

We cannot prove that virtue can be taught. Yet it can be learned through the emulation of those Matthew Arnold called the noble and great who are gone, as we learn how they lived their lives in the histories and biographies we study. For the engaging vividness of legacies recorded, in history and imaginative literature both, is such that it lodges forever in our minds standards of resolution, of allegiance to principle, to country, to friend, that strengthen our conscience, even as we—students in the College—will, by the way we *live,* strengthen our characters, aiding us to resist the fierce blandishments of will. Moreover, such engaging legacies are those of men and women whose lives we may know well enough to understand that, before they were "great," they were like us; that their lives were studded by failure, by error, by self-doubt; and that it was in acknowledging these to be true and by mastering their consequences, learning from them and moving on, that they earned the reputations, the fame of succeeding generations, that was their noblest reward.

The entire tendency of our age is to denigrate and belittle, to attack and ridicule, to trumpet weakness or censure honest failure, to tear down, and to exalt the tinsel ephemera and appurtenances of wealth as the only goals fit to follow by the ablest of our new generation. Rehabilitation from shame comes from selling our "story," because celebrity trumps all.

What counter-example do we have to expose the fraudulence of such a culture and to inspire our students to something greater? We have John Henry Newman's portrait of an English gentleman. It leads Section Ten, Discourse VIII, of *The*

Idea of a University (1852). I may be forgiven for quoting a fair portion of it, and then, debunking it. It is beautiful, but it is not an education for our time:

> Hence it is that it is almost a definition of a gentleman to say he is one who never inflicts pain. This description is both refined and, as far as it goes, accurate. He is mainly occupied in merely removing the obstacles which hinder the free and unembarrassed action of those about him; and he concurs with their movements rather than takes the initiative himself. His benefits may be considered as parallel to what are called comforts or conveniences in arrangements of a personal nature: like an easy chair or a good fire, which do their part in dispelling cold and fatigue, though nature provides both means of rest and animal heat without them. The true gentleman in like manner carefully avoids whatever may cause a jar or a jolt in the minds of those with whom he is cast;—all clashing of opinion, or collision of feeling, all restraint, or suspicion, or gloom, or resentment; his great concern being to make everyone at their ease and at home. He has his eyes on all his company; he is tender towards the bashful, gentle towards the distant, and merciful towards the absurd;... he guards against unseasonable allusions... he is seldom prominent in conversation, and never wearisome....

Later Father Newman calls this description a summary of the lineaments of the ethical character, as they may exist independently of the Grace conferred by the active, unreserved Christian faith.

The definition is so lovely—polished, marmoreal, choicely

eloquent—and its subject, lifeless. It could not have been written after 1914, and on rereading it I thought at once of gentlemen awaiting their deaths, quietly, with arms crooked to assist the ladies into lifeboats, on the *Titanic*. In our own time its answering equivalent might be the computer-generated representation of some sort of morphed ideal man, but a man morphed into nothing except something to admire: a Greek *kouros* from another millennium. Such a man as Newman's gentleman had his use in the world, no doubt, but the idealization warns us that we must be careful in pronouncing the "qualities" we want all our graduates to embody.

We desire virtuous and disinterested citizens and leaders. Subsumed in such a category can be and indeed must be tens of millions of our countrymen. All may share in the qualities of virtue; all may labor to think and to act disinterestedly when they serve in their quality as citizens; and all must discharge their duties as American citizens with the same *gravitas* of my "stiffly patriotic" forbearer, our second president, and indeed of his own son, the polymath John Quincy. Finally, all must (in the motto of the Royal Military College, Sandhurst) Serve to Lead.

But let me provide vivid, *real* examples of the "lineaments" of character and mind both that might distinguish those whom we will prepare, and one day graduate, from the College. Here are three actual Americans of an earlier day, two presented in portraits no less accurate for fastening upon the most admirable lineaments of their subjects, while no doubt ignoring or suppressing the eccentricities, blemishes, and flaws that, somehow, the writers imagined would diminish their subjects' legacies. So far as contemporary American young people are still capable of *emulating*, or of wanting to emulate, the noble and great who are gone, these are affecting enough:

His mind was great and powerful, without being of the very first order; his penetration strong, though not so acute as that of a Newton, Bacon, or a Locke; and as far as he saw, no judgment was ever sounder. It was slow in operation, being little aided by invention or imagination, but sure in conclusion.... He was incapable of fear, meeting personal dangers with the calmest unconcern. Perhaps the strongest feature in his character was prudence, never acting until every circumstance, every consideration, was maturely weighed; refraining if he saw a doubt, but, when once decided, going through with his purpose, whatever obstacles opposed. His integrity was most pure, his justice the most inflexible I have ever known.... He was, indeed, in every sense of the words, a wise, a good, and a great man.

And consider:

Of courage undaunted, possessing a firmness and perseverance of purpose which nothing but impossibilities could divert from its direction, careful as a father of those committed to his charge, yet steady in the maintenance of order and discipline, intimate with the Indian character, customs, and principles, habituated to the hunting life, guarded by exact observation of the vegetables and animals of his own country, against losing time in the description of objects already possessed, honest, disinterested, liberal, of sound understanding and a fidelity to truth so scrupulous that whatever he should report would be as certain as if seen by ourselves, with all these qualifications as if selected and implanted in one body, for this express purpose, I should have no hesitation in confiding the enterprise to him.

Thomas Jefferson wrote both descriptions. We are persuaded of both their ardor and their accuracy, of their writer's determination to do noble but honest service to his task. George Washington and Meriwether Lewis are equally potent in what their memory may yield to their legatees, those who will be students in our College—namely, a plain sense of how character and mind, together, are the irreducible prerequisites of great services rendered to great purposes. It is a melding that two hundred years ago was taken almost for granted in the Americans who sought the most dangerous places on the field. They were not the best and the brightest; they were our wisest and bravest.

Here is another, comparable assessment—this of a man less celebrated than, but in character reminiscent of, both Lewis and William Clark, his friend and colleague. Wallace Stegner describes the intrepid early explorer of the Grand Canyon, John Wesley Powell, who

> had the border education. He had the independence, the confidence, the practical ability to accomplish things that many better men lacked. He did not know enough to be discouraged. The war had given him a lesson in organization and the command of large numbers of men. It had shown him that an amateur soldier could accomplish things as well as many a professional. It had given him a taste for leadership.

Such examples are presented because they powerfully capture what we shall be working to identify, in embryo, in our candidates for enrollment. They embody what idealized portraits can only evoke, and what lists of virtues can only frustrate. The lives of such Americans demonstrate, early in our inquiry, the usefulness of a concept to which our form of education will dedicate much of its effort: a concept toward which every tendency of our flattened egalitarian age is hostile and whose value has long since been abandoned—the concept that lay at the heart of the Founders' idea of what a practical education should be: *emulation.*

In summary: Newman's famous gentleman is an ideal, but he is an ideal incapable of transcending boundaries of time. Our College is not to be the school of the Gentleman (or, Robert, may I say, Lady?), but the school of the American citizen and leader, a place of undergraduate learning, training, living, not without large elements of the traditional substance of liberal education. For our purposes men and exemplars like Washington, Lewis, and Powell are most apt. They represent the fusion of qualities that our culture has put asunder: active and prudent minds *and* the will to act; characters in which the native hue of resolution is not sickli'ed o'er by the pale cast of thought, whose bent is to command not to chatter, to lead not to criticize, to serve not to whine, and to give rather than calculate the cost.

Much later we will consider the academic curriculum appropriate to a college like ours. For now I will say only that, overwhelmingly, its principal nourishment will be found in the study of history (I envision history as being about a third of the curriculum). I do not imply the childlike worship or blind emulation of heroes, but a form of emulation that is earned by serious study and consideration of whole lives—their failures, tragedies, disillusionments, misjudgments and, yes, even crimes, as well as their achievements and legacies; lives resummoned from another age for the instruction of our own, and in the heft and accuracy that the best scholarship may vouchsafe. We will expect our students to be ready to understand and to learn, before they are prompted to dismiss, deconstruct, and desecrate—or before, in compassion and gratitude, they may remember and celebrate. "The troubles of our proud and angry dust," said Housman, "are from eternity, and shall not fail." It is in the lifelong and unceasing consideration of the lives and achievements of those who made and led our country, of nations and cultures not dissimilar from our own, that we may lay up our richest resources for learning to judge, and perhaps to master, the challenges and dangers of our day.

The Founding generation read few literatures and knew little historical scholarship. Like that of the greatest American of the nineteenth century, their reading was far less broad than it was deep. Lincoln learned to write like Lincoln by reading the Bible and Shakespeare. The generation of James Madison and John Adams knew Rome and Greece, the Enlightenment of Europe, and the Bible. They read Greek and Latin. They, themselves, saw the struggles of political men through the lenses of writers determined to locate and extol lessons—in wisdom, virtue, patriotism. They did learn, and master, and remember, lessons of conduct that truly influenced the ways in which they lived their lives and led our country. They came to the study of the life of Pericles or of Cato like Jay Gatsby came to a new acquaintance: with an overwhelming prejudice in the person's favor, not with a cynic's determination to find the disqualifying or unknown flaw of character or mistake of judgment— and I trust that some, at least, of that overwhelming prejudice in favor of men and women long gone, who have deserved well of their country, still remains.

Dear Robert,

From time to time a friend of mine, a professor at the University of Wyoming, wonders idly what Tocqueville, were he alive, would notice about the Way We Live Now. No one knew us better—our *métier*, our peculiar *ethos*, the perfectly predictable persistence of our character. The prognoses of no other commentator, foreign or homegrown, have been more fully vindicated. He knew us as Xenophon knew Athens, as Pepys knew London. He knew what we were *like*; to give him his highest American due, what he wrote, you could take to the bank.

He would note still our terrible restlessness and dissatisfaction with whatever we have earned or achieved; the fury of our motion, the desperation of our pursuit of the appurtenances of status and of celebrity—highest among these the simulacra of youth and the coincident exaltation of medical doctors (and, by the way, my own physician was here an hour ago and assured me I could maintain quality of life for another four months anyway, thus, in his words, "validating my hope"). He would watch fascinatedly all the television advertising about people trying to remain young and perfectly healthy in all ways, particularly including their ability to achieve regular movement of their bowels. And he would study, his instincts confirmed, the epiphenomena of our pathetic need for approval of the kind that parades an unassailable specificity tricked out with rankings: fourth runners-up, third-place finishers, Final Fours, Top Tens, Oscar nominations, and the rest. A neighbor's grandchild appeared the other day to thank me for a note I had written on her behalf to a university whose name it would be ungracious of me to mention, and which, she told me, was now "ranked fifth"; and, when challenged, she produced the ranking authority, an annual production of *U.S. News & World Report,* devoted to a study of "The Nation's Best Colleges." (The year before the university had "ranked seventh," so that the child's admission was now doubly to be felicitated, and her parents' delight scarcely to be imagined. Fifth!)

A kind of numerical compost heap is built up, a bouillabaisse of data concocted, the vital ingredients of which would seem to be the mean SATs of those offered admission and those who "actually enroll," and the assessed quality of academic offerings provided by the various departments and majors. Other numbers and data are adduced, the usual fustian, rather like Henry VIII's factitious justifications for taking over the Church in England, the church that has become today's sloppy agoppy church, in phrases like "whereas by diverse old authentic histories," and so on. Since the mean SAT is 1430 recentered, and since 90 percent of the entering class were in the top X percent of the graduating classes in the high schools, now, therefore, we award you the ranking of seventh, no, fifth....

The utility of such practices is zero. No, worse than zero. Everything that we should value and exalt in the way we educate our young people in college is ignored utterly; or if not ignored, forgotten or unknown. What kinds of men and women teach the students? What do they teach them? For what have such numbers, such rankings, to do with what the undergraduates will become when they are forty or sixty? Asserting that College X "ranks" ninth regionally is like writing that Professor Jones has published seventy-one papers, or that University Z has "produced twenty-one Rhodes scholars" (as though the university were a salmon hatchery). What if sixty of the papers are stupid or wrong? What if nine of the Rhodes scholars are drunks?

I found (certain mathematicians excepted) that no one I hired for the company whose work was truly first-class had scores such as those imputed to the graduates of the fifth-ranking university in the land, and that the qualities of character that our colleges ought to labor to train, to instill, to help educate, were less likely to be found among these high-powered tyros (whose ranks the little girl now joins) than in a quiet, steady graduate of a tiny school in the Kentucky Outback who went to chapel, studied Latin, and went back to New Carthage to marry the kid who sat next to her in the eighth grade.

Anyway, Tocqueville would notice this as surely as, with a snaggle of mirth both derisory and tolerant, he would see, on the right bumper of the RV passing him on U.S. 50, a sticker avowing that, beyond dispute, the owner's daughter is AN HONOR STUDENT AT HARDING MIDDLE SCHOOL.

Your affectionate friend,
John Adams

CHAPTER 3

Who Should They Be?

"Whom shall I send, and who will go for us?"

The response, in Isaiah VI, is as simple as it is uncalculated.

"Here am I. Send me."

I LOVE THE QUALITY OF ARDOR, and I never see it anymore. We must look for it in those young people who will be our candidates for admission: ardor for opportunity, its demands and difficulties granted and understood. Our selection committees will recognize it when they see it. Those who want what we offer, partly because of their age, partly *in spite* of the age, will not be comparison shoppers.

But I am far ahead of myself.

I have said we will be a residential college, and that our students will be undergraduates. Laying deeply the habits of a certain kind of living (which has nothing to do with what is called "lifestyle") will require that our students be *at* the College, subject to its regimen and its expectations. Again, I have put a useful size for us as 1,200—boys and girls. And they will be boys and girls, not young men and young women, when we find, examine, select, appoint, and enroll them: high school students of *junior* standing, ordinarily fifteen or sixteen years of age. The net size of the studentry will be about 1,500—Cohort IV, the fourth-year members of a five-year course, will be away for almost all that academic year.

We are looking for young people who possess qualities of mind and character that will suit them for our course of education. I am certain that such qualities are not reliably disclosed by the instruments currently employed by our most competitive universities. Nor are they disclosed by the various testing agencies that do so much of the assessing, the "screening," of candidates. Such practices and those who engage in them are not suited to our enterprise. They have become but the fashionable means by which well-satisfied institutions further aggrandize their reputations, their cachet. The fact is that the Scholastic Aptitude Test, class rank, IQ results, grades, lists of extracurricular activities, forced accounts of "transforming experiences" assembled as required essays, and all the accompanying objects that overwhelm committees on admission—these are near to worthless for our purposes, no better than sledgehammers for cutting diamonds or boxing gloves for playing Mozart. What we are looking for is a compound of practical intelligence, mother wit, determination, courage, certain early signs of selflessness, and a demonstrated willingness to go against the grain of expectation. I maintain that these qualities are not so latent that they cannot be identified among fifteen- or sixteen-year-olds.

What we want is an admixture of mettle and demonstrated independence of judgment and character, a habit of autonomy already ingrained in a few young people. It discloses itself in any number of ways, one of them being a passionate attachment to some intellectual (or musical or artistic) interest that provides no "reward" but the joy and satisfaction it gives the student. He is not, that is, doing something for a grade or a resumé or to gratify an ambitious parent. We want students who transcend circumstances of birth, and to some extent circumstances of (what was once called) upbringing. I might for example argue that almost any group of adults, randomly chosen from a community and a variety of professions, would have had little trouble in sensing—recognizing—in the fifteen-year-old Harry Truman those qualities and potentials of character that would qualify him for posts of leadership much later on. However sissified, however "soft" in appearance, however contrary the superficial characteristics of his personality might have seemed, he provided the early signs: his long bouts of private reading in thick histories of Roman and American revolutionary history, his long sessions of practice at the piano, his thoroughness in discharging menial duties. He would certainly have manifested this essential thing we must identify in our own successful candidates.

I associate it with strong intellect, but not necessarily the kind of intellect that excels academically. Wisdom of the sort we want in our graduates is not reliably correlated with academic excellence. It may be, it may not be. One of its largest components, obviously, is what Howard Gardner calls the "Personal Intelligences," the ability to "read," to understand the character and motivations of others—an ability that is rarely disclosed on academic tests.

Let me give a tiny, homely example before proceeding on.

In 1952 a boy was accepted for admission at Yale. He was among several admitted from a school in New England. The boy's scores and grades were only average.

His father asked the Yale admissions dean why the man had accepted him. Later he committed the dean's response to his diary. It is most instructive and pertinent:

When I visited the school in February I interviewed several candidates, one of them your son. He was quiet, had good manners, and looked directly at me, not saying much. That afternoon I went to a hockey game. I noticed several applicants to Yale were on the team. Your son was the goalie, and he played well. I remember that when his application came in, a few weeks later, I noticed that he played catcher on the baseball team, and also that he was an All-State center in football.

I had a moment of modest epiphany. Your son played the three positions—goalie, center, catcher—that were most dangerously exposed, most taken for granted, from which quiet influence and leadership are most importantly originated in these sports, in which the possibility of a mistake leading to disaster is largest, and to which least attention is given when victory results. I thought to myself, isn't this exactly the kind of boy we want here?—assuming he can do the academic work. Hasn't he shown already that he has what Yale should be in business to educate? It was apparent to me that the smartest boys we are admitting will one day look to the likes of your son for leadership, for steadiness of direction, selflessness, and courage.

In the judgment of the admissions dean (and this was a long time ago) the boy would be able to do the academic work required for graduation. He was sufficiently "smart" to attain the necessary academic success, and indeed that hard-won success would itself be a reliable testimony both to his self-discipline and to his conditioned ability to work hard and long, and alone, and to complete difficult assignments. It is this trained ability that is as likely to grow to what may become wisdom in the world of affairs as is verbal acuity of the sort that leads to high scores on such instruments of academic prediction as the Verbal SAT. It is the accompaniment of a patient, probably unself-conscious, practice of watching and studying others, and of quietly learning about their motivations and frustrations. Those whose academic knowledge is hard-earned are often much better at this than the quick and clever.

Character and the potential to attain wisdom are what we

are looking for. And we must decide how to go about locating such things in those who will be candidates for admission to our College.

I argue first that such judgments are most reliably made, not by a committee of university professors and administrators (embodied, with admissions "professionals," as a Committee on Admission), but by ordinary citizens who have achieved a measure of success in their professions, and who are known, too, for their own civic or avocational interests and contributions. I trust the judgments of such people, not excluding the role that intuition plays in them, with greater confidence than I heed the assessments of so-called experts in college admission. Lord Salisbury's dictum was never more pertinent than here: "Nothing is so deeply inculcated by the experience of life as that you must never trust experts." The word to attend to, of course, is not so much "experts" as it is "trust."

For my interest is in what the young candidates are going to be like when they are thirty or fifty, rather than in how well suited they may be to achieving academic excellence. All should pursue such excellence, of course; no one argues that. But I am struck, repeatedly and forcibly, by the extraordinary careers and achievements—especially in government, business, science, music, politics, military service, and the ministries of faith—of people whose academic achievements in college were meager, and whose "test scores were low."

Emphatically, we should not exclude possible geniuses in any field of enterprise or talent. The idea that a great artist, for example, should not "go to" an ordinary college strikes me as idiotic—as idiotic as his school curriculum may have struck him, which may account for his grades and "test scores." Nor must we overlook or ignore the lazy, "difficult" youngster. Here is where certain kinds of appointments to our committees on admission can be particularly useful: men and women used to watching young people in their natural habitats, which are not necessarily schools. Here certain individual, discrete incidents can be enormously helpful to us. "I suddenly saw that he..."—such an observation from a career secondary schoolteacher or a scoutmaster may disclose something more useful to our purpose than a raft of test scores and class rankings. I know, further, that as an accolade and predictor of likely future usefulness to the commonweal, the achievement of an Eagle Scout rank (what is the female equivalent?) is a far more relevant predictor than a high Math SAT. More helpful than either, of course, is detailed evidence that candidates have, in difficult situations, followed the dictates of conscience, in the absence of incentive, positive sanction, and, even more impressive, with the possibility looming of some form of reprisal. As James McGregor Burns said in his book on leadership, "...a test of adherence to 'values' is the willingness to apply principles or standards to oneself as well as to others."

In what circumstances will our applicants, our candidates, have grown up? Were they, for example, home-schooled? Were they raised in poverty or luxury, in slums or stylish suburbs, on remote, almost self-sustaining farms or in cities? What kinds of hazards and dangers will they have surmounted?

The key is to assess native talent, character, and mind while "controlling for" circumstances not of a student's own making. One child is hurried to Suzuki classes beginning at four; another, hearing the word, probably thinks Suzuki is a 9 mm weapon. One child comes to consciousness in a world of mild and accommodating circumstances; another in an unheated apartment without a loving parent. One goes to a good school, the other.... And yet, the signs, the markers of a certain resisting independence of temperament, of the potential for "character," for avid learning, will survive in the candidates we want, hardy as scrub pine on a windblown ridgeline. Our committees on selection must find it, recognize it, reward it.

Further, I don't believe candidates for admission whose written records and recommendations testify to perfect happiness and unblemished successes through childhood and early adolescence are as likely to qualify for our mission as children who have had to surmount obstacles of various kinds, and who have already known failures—young as they are. We know that ultimately the "key to heroic character is not the absence of failure but rather resilience in the face of defeat." "It is said," wrote the most famous Englishman of our dying century, and one of the two greatest men of action his country ever produced, "that famous men are usually the product of an unhappy childhood. The stern compression of circumstances, the twinges of adversity, the spur of slights and taunts in early years, are needed to evoke that ruthless fixity of purpose and tenacious mother wit without which great actions are seldom accomplished." The author is writing of his great ancestor the Duke of Marlborough; he was obviously thinking about himself, Winston Churchill. Indeed he could have been writing about a child, now fourteen, being ridiculed for wearing a uniform prescribed by his parochial school as he makes his way through a neighborhood where such insigne excites immediate censure—perhaps because he is "acting white."

As for that, what is called affirmative action is to have no part in our identification of prospective candidates and students. First, because I disbelieve in what "affirmative action" has become—however noble its early purpose. Second, because it has no relevance to our methodology. For all I know, our first cohort will have 250 black girls. Gender and race are not criteria for assessment, except in unusual circumstances that conspire to teach us something particular about a candidate.

The Selection and Enrollment of Candidates

How should the process work?

Since ours is to be a five-year undergraduate college of about 1,500, each entering cohort should comprise some three hundred freshmen, perhaps a few more. They are to be drawn from all American states, the minimum from each being two, the maximum seven. I am not persuaded that this is unfair to California or Texas—very large states—given that their populations are larger by many magnitudes than those of, say, New Hampshire and Montana. The larger good is that all parts of the country are represented substantially; cultural and other variances among candidate backgrounds are accentuated. Were we to populate the College by calculations of population density only, we would deprive those enrolled from what I take to be an important feature of what we will be offering: the chance to live among those in many ways not like ourselves, but Americans, citizens of the American Republic, all the same.

Though the College may one day become famous (or perhaps infamous), and though it may one day excite an avid competition for admission (not to mention its "free" education), I believe it must search initially for prospective candidates *who do not know they are being considered.* I suppose word will leak, but that leakage can, with some care, be reduced.

There should be embodied in every state, soon after Labor Day, a committee of ten or twelve men and women, adults representing a variety of professions or avocations (see below). The person calling the assembly should be some eminent, nonpolitical person of known probity and stature in each state capital. (One possibility, in the selection of conveners, is to rotate the appointment among priests, rabbis, ministers, and so on, of the major religious denominations in the capital.) This person will have visited the College and learned its mission and character, its curriculum, and the requirements for candidates, in detail; one assumes he or she will have become a convinced adherent of its purposes. We will provide necessary logistical support, as well as the proverbial modest honorarium.

He would be responsible for attracting and gathering nominations of prospective candidates from all over his state, from among the ranks of that state's high school *juniors*, or those of equivalent standing—from a variety of local and county sources: principals, heads of service agencies and scouting organizations, ministers, officials in the towns. He might communicate with nominators as follows:

A New American College

A new College, to open in August 2000, seeks to identify high school juniors most suited to enrollment at the school. Its purpose is the preparation of virtuous and disinterested citizens and leaders for the Republic. Criteria for admission differ from those used by colleges and universities to which your students now make application; the means by which the College will assess a candidate's fitness and aptness for admission will differ also. The College will enroll undergraduates only, for a five-year program, its academic curriculum to embody some requirements traditional to liberal education, but others (for example, the mastery to fluency of two foreign languages, one of them non-Western; required courses in mathematics, logic, and deontology) less apt to be required in contemporary undergraduate curricula. Eighteen months of the five-year tenure will be spent away from the College's demesne, which is currently being readied near Douglas, Wyoming. All costs of the full undergraduate program, including tuition, room, board, books and sundries, and travel costs, will be borne by the College. All graduates are to incur a three-year obligation for service in some agency of federal, state, or local government. Principal qualifications for admission comprise, among others, demonstrated qualities of self-reliance, selflessness, tenacity, integrity, and judgment. The College is uninterested in matters of race, gender, or religious provenance; and such considerations therefore form no part of its admissions activity.

Please send to the _____ State Committee, c/o The Rev'd _____, Main Street, USA, the names of possible candidates and a brief description of each. Do not, even if known, include SAT, ACT, or IQ "scores."

A significant burden is thus laid on those from whom we will solicit nominations. Our state convener, on behalf of the committee, will ask nominators to present further evidence of their candidates' fitness for consideration and eventual admission. I would leave the preliminary evaluation of these evidences up to him, trusting to his understanding that we want to see things other than (or, later, in addition to) the usual commendations of grades, class rank, "essays," awards, National Merit Commendations, and so on.

Suppose that each committee selects twelve candidates from among those nominated—selects, that is, for invitations to a residence of five or six days, in some comfortable retreat site, there to live among members of the committee on selection. They are not invited so much to be "interviewed," a word and an event which both terrifies many candidates and may for trivial reasons skew the result; as to be, over a long period of time, quietly evaluated and assessed—judged—but in ways which rather searchingly act to find out what the candidates are really "like." A long and leisured time together seems to me necessary. St. Chrysostom says in his *Treatise on the Priesthood*, "Public report often speaks false; but when careful investigation precedes, no further danger need be apprehended from it…. [The selector] does not dispense with an exact and rigorous inquiry, nor does he assign to such testimony precedence over the scrutiny required in such cases."

A typical state committee, called together at some central location for a week's work in our behalf, might comprise the following:

1. A homemaker. Almost certainly a woman. Not less than forty-five years old, and with at least one child of each sex not less than twenty.
2. A sitting municipal court judge.
3. A retired high school principal less than five years removed from his retirement.
4. A scientist or an inventor.
5. A medical doctor in general practice.
6. A sports journalist.
7. A farmer.
8. A retired U.S. congressman or senator.
9. An artisan.

10. A clergyman.
11. The chief operating officer of a company he founded himself.

I don't think these selections need much commentary. Together they seem to me to unite qualities of sound and penetrating judgment about young people, abilities cultivated through experience and reflection. A cynic or a sophisticate might smile at such an assembly, just as a surgeon might scorn the phrase "ordinary citizen" as denoting a man without an earned portfolio. But a lifetime spent among ordinary citizens of my country—in settings and enterprises as diverse as those of combat in wartime, *pro bono* activity on church and university boards, appointed federal positions, and forty years in business, most with the same company, of which I was the founder—convinces me that the most reliable judgments of the kind we need are made by ordinary people and citizens. A tugboat captain in New York harbor is to my mind a better judge of character than a college admissions gunsel, running around the preparatory circuit with an eye cocked to SATs and APs, all aimed at "Ratings Surveys" that measure the value of a college by standards that ignore the most important things of all: great teaching, for example. Character. Determination. My list comprises men and women who in their ordinary lives continually have to make judgments about character. They know what it means.

Who is likely a better judge of character than general practitioners or farmers, given the exigencies of professions that depend on factors that cannot usually be controlled by human agency? And who would be more likely to understand motivation, sincerity, the capacity for redemption or for moral growth, than a long-sitting judge or a high school principal? Who would be more difficult to mislead than men and women in such posts? A high school principal or headmaster (invariably an experienced teacher) who has given thirty years to secondary education will have unconsciously cultivated an uncanny intuition about what young people are likely to become—about which bored sophomore is almost certain, in an environment like that of our new College, to be transformed into an extraordinarily useful and admirable citizen and leader, whatever his own profession will be.

Some of our other committee members, these ordinary men and women who have made extraordinary lives for themselves and their communities, need little comment. A sports journalist, given what professional athletics has become, has a peculiarly well-adapted field of study of human character. A scientist or an inventor will bring to the work a keen intuition for possible, heretofore undisclosed capacities for original thought in candidates whose records may be merely mediocre. As for our retired member of Congress, I see him (or her) now no longer struggling in the arena, and perhaps unusually willing to seek out young, determined idealists.

Memorandum on Admission: Considerations for Members of Selection Committees

[Note: This note was attached to Adams's "Who Should They Be?" essay on admission to the College. It is a useful amplification of his views on the subject. R.P.]

WE HAVE STATED THE MISSION. We are preparing a curriculum, molding an *ethos*, for the life of the College, to serve that mission. These force the obvious question: given the mission, on what bases do committees on selection make their choices? Among candidates nominated, who will be aptest for our purpose?

A certain kind of "brilliant" brain is no particular commendation to us, unless it is lodged in a certain kind of character, and unless accompanied by other qualities of a moral nature. The kind of brain I want us to avoid is the one that industriously has swotted up loads of information on assigned topics, with ambitious but passive industry, and that has trained itself to deliver responses it senses are wanted, by tests, questioners, and the like. I call such brains downloaders; they are not of interest. As for verbal facility as measured on standardized testing instruments, it is useful and for some professions necessary, but the assessing of the inborn and cultivated ability to make superfine discriminations among words, and clever analogical inferences and parsings, has become nothing more than a gulling fetish for test-takers and admissions offices, to be rewarded with "high scores" that indicate... but what? What do they indicate? "Phthisical is to Etiolated as Puce is to (a) Amber (b) Ocher (c) Madder (d) Mauve." Such an ability is useful to those who excel in crossword puzzles, or in the writing of a certain kind of literary criticism, and perhaps, sometimes, "at law"; beyond this it is of no particular commendation to us.

Again: take the chance on the girl or boy of relatively meager SAT performance, and high grades, or evidences of independent intellectual or artistic achievement, in preference to the opposite.

I do not see academic cleverness as an especially useful commodity for those intending to be people of affairs. When I was at Cambridge, sent there after my last year at the University of Chicago, I met dozens of third- and fourth-year undergraduates of whom others said, in awe and reverence, that they would leave with double firsts in Greek and philosophy, and that they would surely go into the Treasury or the Foreign Office. Meeting them, all I could think of was Munich.

Be wary of academic cleverness. Be wary of rigid academic industriousness. Look rather for evidences of determination, perseverance, the willingness to take risks, independence of judgment, the habit of hard, sustained watchfulness and listening, for quirky expertises privately cultivated, for incidents of *challenging* received opinions or the authoritativeness of teachers' pronouncements. Look for unexpected answers to questions you may pose during discussions with candidates. I remember vividly an essay written by a candidate, a girl, for admission to a university on whose board I then sat. The question was supremely asinine: "Describe honors and awards that you have won." To this fatuity the child responded: "I am surprised and disappointed that a university such as yours would allow the inclusion of such a question, among the various means employed to judge my qualification for enrollment. Do you seriously think the kind of person you want pays any attention to 'honors and awards'? Consider this answer my withdrawal from active candidacy for admission to the university...."

[Adams has written in pencil at the bottom of the memorandum: "Like boys who have played contact sports. Candidates who look right at you while they are giving answers. If wearing leather shoes see if backs are shined as well as front." R.P.]

We are considering lines of inquiry and investigation that will disclose habits of mind, independence of temper, qualities of thoughtfulness that seem to unite intellection with practical application; I set down also other characteristics that our committees should look for, if only for early or small evidences of them—remembering, again, that our candidates are only fifteen or sixteen years of age:

1. Unself-conscious moral courage.
2. Self-forgetfulness.
3. Indifference to material success and to "things."
4. Fierce patriotism.
5. Willingness to assume responsibility without calculation of reward or risk.
6. Intellectual self-reliance and independence of judgment.
7. Retention of a lifelong sense of wonder.
8. Magnanimity; liberality; generosity of temper.
9. Physical hardihood and resistance to fatigue.

One may object that such things should be aims, not qualifications: qualities for which we will *educate* pupils, not for which they should be selected. How can we expect American adolescents of our time, or any time after 1900, to be indifferent to material success, or to be self-forgetful, or fiercely patriotic? I have but a modest expectation that most of our candidates will give clear evidence of such things, but a few will; and the capacity to be educated toward such things may declare itself in other ways. It is for the committees to search for them. They should be especially alert, in their researches and scrutiny of records, letters of testimonial, conversations with adults who know the candidates, *to singular acts of courage moral and physical*; and where there are testimonials to such acts from the candidates' own contemporaries, so much more are they to be attended to. There is great cruelty in the behavior of adolescents toward each other; wariness and tension between the races; much discomfort around eccentricity and, equally, a constant and ill-disguised obsession with conforming. Who among our nominated candidates will have demonstrated an early capacity to act against these grains? Who will have shown the force of character to stand up for what his heart and conscience tell him is right, consequences be damned?

Be wary of letters of reference prepared by adults who are obvious partisans of the candidates' ambitions for this opportunity—be alert to certain words, phrases, of reiterated generality, obvious euphemisms, tired litanies of educationist palaver. I have seen that when referees (for jobs in the company as well as places in the university) use the phrase "modest gifts," they mean either that the candidate is irredeemably stupid or that he has average academic abilities but such formidable habits of work and concentration that he is to be preferred to "more gifted" candidates who have done little with their abilities. It is amusing how much we can learn from people who, in writing one thing about a candidate, are communicating precisely the opposite. It is lamentable that many of those asked to prepare references for candidates barely *know* them—and sometimes, literally, do not, *viz*, "Although I have not personally met Louise, I have known her Uncle Michael for many years, and...."

I want candidates to remain in residence with committee members for five or six days, in settings that allow all to come to know each other, and that will amplify quite radically the normal process of essay and interview—and that will break down the artificial barriers that are set up in such circumstances. There must be times for long talks, and even on occasion discussions that are in outward form "interviews," but that the students may not feel to be such.

Assuming state committees make their selections by late September and that selectees notify the College by October 1 of their decision to accept or not to accept our offer of admission, membership in the following fall's cohort should be fixed by mid-October. There are thus almost ten months between admission and enrollment—time that should be used carefully by the College to assure a standard of minimal preparation by all entering students. In our academic calendar as I envision it, August is a month given to orientation for first-year students (and used by other cohorts for a variety of purposes). One feature of the August orientation will be a thorough grounding in all computer usages—each entering student will be given a laptop at the time of admission. But I propose some sort of diagnostic test be administered *after* enrollment, in order to determine proficiency in mathematics and English, so that we may arrange some remedial support at the student's local high school or elsewhere, if needed, before matriculation at the College. In addition, each student's principal mentor—assigned almost immediately after students are selected—will then begin a correspondence with him, in which he describes the College's aims, curriculum, living circumstances, and the rest, and develops a friendship with the student. *This* mentor will be our student's principal advisor during his years at the College, and during his times away from it during interims, the language abroad program, and his military (and other) service.

We should also require entering students to read the following: Daniel Defoe, *Robinson Crusoe*; Francis Parkman, *The Oregon Trail*; Stephen E. Ambrose, *Custer and Crazy Horse*; Ian Frazier, *The Great Plains*; Gretel Erlich, *The Solace of Open Spaces*; David Herbert Donald, *Lincoln*; and Plato, *The Apology of Socrates*. I select these with the obvious purpose of introducing our new students to their future environs, and to three Americans, very different from one another, who when young determined to *make* themselves leaders—and because these books are immediately engaging. In general I oppose stunning young students with opening questions and topics of a profound and abstract character, *viz*, "What Is Truth?" "What Is the Nature of Being?", and so on. At some point during his five years at the College, every student will read *The Republic*, *The Peloponnesian War*, *War and Peace*, Locke's *Second Treatise*, and such mighty classics; but not now.

Forgive me for getting ahead of myself.

The periods when prospective students are in residence must be so contrived that committee members are able to observe candidates without the latter knowing that they are being observed; and that a variety of practical (or moral) problems, tests, and so forth, be offered them. I hasten to say that I do not mean observation in a physical way, or in a way that abridges the candidates' privacy; I mean, rather, such things as these:

Four candidates are in the lobby of the main building of a retreat center or resort. They have just arrived, have been

dropped off, and are about to check in. Two or three committee members advance to greet them. An alarm goes off in the
lobby and a clerk announces a bomb threat: probably, he says, in
the main dining room adjacent to the lobby—on the other side
of the lobby, that is, from the entrance way. How do the candidates *react*? Which if any asks immediately, "Is anyone in that
room?" Which if any runs to check the dining room?

Or: several candidates, on occupying their rooms, find wallets
or purses left by earlier guests, each with identification and pho-
tos—and each also with, say, a fifty-dollar bill, two twenties, and
a ten. Which occupants report the missing wallets? Which turn
them in with all the money?

Or: a group of candidates is given three hours to get from
one site to another, with some difficulties or obstacles obtrud-
ing. Since one of the College's principal means of helping students learn leadership will be to *require* them to lead small
groups across long stretches of the western High Plains and the
Laramies and Big Horn Mountains, this whiff of what lies ahead
may provide valuable clues to the resourcefulness of various candidates. What we are looking for, of course, are clear brains, but
also a sense of how to translate diagnosis into prescription, and
then into action, particularly when it requires that others be
led in the doing. In turn, after such small group challenges,
individual members may be asked to evaluate one another—and
in scrutinizing what they have to say about each other we will
learn more about their characters and intelligence than about
those whom they are evaluating. In such requirements we can
discover candidates' determination and fellow feeling.

And I think before our candidates left (I imagine each state
would have invited about twelve to fifteen for residence), I'd ask
each of them to write and tell us why he wants to become a

member of the College—what it is, from what he will have seen and heard and learned about it, that makes him respond, ardently and ambitiously, to the opportunity.

No sooner—certainly—than two weeks after the retreat with our candidates, the convener should reassemble the committee to consider the candidates' qualifications for appointment to the College. The two weeks is important. It will allow for thoughtful consideration of the dossiers that we will have assembled on each of them, and of the portfolios the candidates will have been asked to assemble in their own behalfs. It will allow for long conversations among committee members, and between members and the referees (I should think each candidate might be asked to provide at least three names, of teachers, coaches, church leaders, and the like). It will allow time for members to visit candidates in their homes, to learn more about their lives, their families, and their neighborhoods. The time will allow also for impressions to settle and to take useful shape, for intuition and reflection to leaven evidence, and for first impressions (normally wrong in this kind of enterprise) to be amended.

Depending on the state, our committees will select between two and seven young people to join the College as members of Cohort I.

Now, Robert, that is how the admission procedure and process might work. Does it make any sense to you? Or do you think that we are trying to locate a certain potential that cannot be judged in those so young? Or do you think we are about to recruit a platoon of Boy Scouts and goody-goodies who, whatever kinds of citizens they may be, hold little real potential for leadership? To the skepticism I impute to you and everyone else (because I have had these conversations with friends for many years), I respond: *it has never really been tried before.* I believe we have a chance of making our pupils not only wiser and per-haps even braver but also *better*. And I believe that the very early evidences of that capability—to become better—are plain to those who look for them; and, I cannot resist adding, particu-larly in young people who have grown up in circumstances you and I would call difficult: in the ghettos of the inner cities of our country, in circumstances of poverty and deprivation wherever we encounter them—in circumstances, in short, where some few young persons will have already demonstrated that they know how to make their *own* opportunities, and in so doing have not forgotten their friends, either.

*D*EAR MR. ADAMS,

Thank you for the two sections. Thank you also for your letter speculating about Tocqueville's reaction to contemporary culture. You ask, "What is our mission?", and you ask, "What students should be enrolled in the College?" My mission is to convene the five members of the foundation board—the managers of your committed money—and prepare them for their transition to members of the founding board of your College. I understand from the first part of "What Is Our Mission?" that I may expect the last three sections of your proposal (blueprint? fixed plan?) over the next few months. Then we will begin the laborious work of converting an idea into a reality. Exhilarating to you, laborious (as well as exhilarating) to the rest of your associates!

I have two children. They both want to go to Brown; they both have SATs in the high 1400s. One wants to be an anthropologist, and the other, a screenwriter. I have discreetly mentioned your work to the eldest, Ashley, and she recommends you make all your candidates take the Raven Progressive Matrices examination. It assesses abstract reasoning ability, and it controls for culture, environment, and family circumstance. If you saw it, and I will fax it to you, you'd recognize it as an old-fashioned spatial relationships assessment instrument. I have taken it in sample form and have not excelled.

I look forward to your next chapter. I trust you are feeling better. Surely you can keep your beast at bay, weaken him, and slay him. In this connection I am sending a piece from the Boston Globe on a new protocol they are promoting at Sloan-Kettering, more-or-less precisely applicable to your kind of cancer.

Permit me to observe that it is possible to be very smart and also to have character. And also to be a patriot. I cannot think of anyone who proves my point better than the men about whom you quote in your first chapter. Would you not say the Founding generation proves my point?

The full portfolio, less anticipated fees and a few changes at the margin and also less the $175 million allowed for construction, easement, architects, consultants, and so on, invested according to total return practices, should yield not less than $42 million per annum.

Yours sincerely,
Robert Parkman

My daughter says Chicago has no flair, no jeu d'esprit, *which is why she wants to go to Brown.*

M<small>Y DEAR</small> R<small>OBERT</small>,

I have labored over these pages for some weeks: "How Should They Live?" Quietly abide the small narrative, near the beginning, about how I came to love the High Plains, and why the College is to be in Wyoming.

There is a big wind howling desperately away, gathering and regathering itself in a kind of insatiable voracity, as though, almost, it were trying to tear the tattered trees off the mountains, and the roofs off our houses. In this El Niño winter it is a dry, snowless wind. It will not exhaust itself until mid-April. The incongruity is large. It is late at night. I am tucked up in my study. I am, just slightly, buoyed by a new radiologist's report. And I have only now heard the name "Monica Lewinsky." I wonder whether it will register in the national consciousness, and become famous, iconographic—like, say, Ralph Branca or Howard Hunt? I have a new biography of John Quincy Adams lying open on my lap, and I have just rewritten the small section on "parietals," certain rules connected to visiting among men and women in each other's rooms and houses. Most colleges no longer have parietals; if they do, they are so absurdly hedged and so diffidently, begrudgingly enforced that they are worthless. I have insisted that in our College such rules be strait and enforced. Their purpose, mainly, is to keep the sexes apart in their dormitories. I once heard a woman, the wife of a headmaster, tell a reporter that "our mission is to keep them off drugs, and off each other." She did not apologize for her view. Our mission in this regard is to stand for something. I know that my expectation will be challenged and disappointed from time to time, as it is everywhere else. But I ask, is that a reason to drop the rules or requirements?

Three years ago I rotated off (that is the term of art) the board of a college in Ohio. At my last meeting I went into a men's room in the student center. There was a condom dispenser affixed to the wall, over a row of urinals, and the device might have been at a gas station on an interstate in Tennessee! Each brand, or rather, *style*, of condom depicted a young woman, her face contorted by a laborious pleasure, and the condoms were described as configured in different ways in order to make for a "heightened" sensation. The absurdity is (I'm not that much of a prude) as funny as it is lamentable. Here was our university, which had "produced" twelve Rhodes scholars and two Trumans, flat-out hawking instruments of sexual pleasure, in the name of safety from venereal disease. (The same school regularly "made available" rubber dams for undergraduates who "requested" them. I tried to envisage the scene: the fey undergraduate "requesting" a "rubber dam" from his [or her] residence assistant? infirmary nurse? Your country, Robert.)

I do not know who Monica Lewinsky is. I love her name. The superheated *Eyewitness News* Authority Person disappears, and the American president succeeds him, his voice a mass of demiquavers and his eyes oscillant sideways, pronouncing, in his ginned-up, measured way, "There is no improper sexual relationship," or some such "I'll not dignify that outrageous suggestion by any further...." We are so very far from TR, from Lincoln, from (indeed) John Quincy Adams. We no longer expect to be led by such men. They would not run; and if they did, "we" would not elect them, because they took thus-and-such a position on thus-and-such, and we can't have that. A poll is adduced—information that shows the American people don't care about the sexual allegations against the president; they are secure in their persons, they are tired, they are happy with their

RVs, their IRAs, their lawnboys, Britas, faxes, record Dow Joneses, and the sight of their big carriers purling up and down the Persian Gulf, manned and womaned by other men's children. Celebrities fool around, and unemployment is at 4.5 percent. Hey, what's the problem?

The raffish behavior of our public men is like the antics of the Greek gods, and we are by now conditioned to take them precisely as such: that is how they are, and there is little signification in their behavior for us.

Just now they are showing an alligator briefcase that belonged to John Kennedy....

I have been asleep for ninety minutes. I have read through my pages again. The scale of what we will be doing is so small, but that should neither daunt our conviction nor make us apologetic. The Lord's best work is always done in the smallest compass, not in the largest or most famous. We shall this day, light such a fire in England as, I trust... were they still teaching that by the time you got to the university, Robert?

With warmest regards,

John Adams

CHAPTER 4

How Should They Live?

HERE WE HAVE TO DESCRIBE THE CIRCUMSTANCES of our students' lives during the five years they are members of the College. How they are to live is at the center of our work. Though it is not where academic instruction is ordinarily provided, it is where most real learning occurs: learning as intellectual as all that any syllogism or book, scholar or formula, may hope to demonstrate, prove, or propound. It is the aspect of the undergraduate experience that our best colleges conspicuously, if shamefacedly, ignore; or, when they cannot ignore it, in which they most fecklessly intervene, always spasmodically and irritably, as though they deserved better from students who are, they explain, very "bright."

There is much for us to address.

Where will our College be? How will our students *live*, organize themselves (with our help), and attend to various extra-academic needs and obligations? What should those obligations be? How can we contrive the circumstances of their lives that we may help equip them with the habits of virtuous and disinterested conduct we should expect of our best citizens and leaders? What for our purposes are appropriate means of teaching honorable conduct? What sort of calendar and schedule should the College have? And what of the relations between the sexes? What use are we to make of the peculiar circumstances of the College's natural situation? How will the community, of *all* persons living at the College, be sustained? There are dozens of such questions to be answered.

I have lived all over our country and, briefly, abroad. I grew up on the edge of a heartland city of medium size—Decatur, Illinois. My parents gave me what seems to have been a normal midwestern boyhood for the 1930s, rounding it off (such was my father's expression) by sending me east to boarding school, to a gentle ambling place, sweet and humane rather than puritanically tense, near Princeton. But for only a year. And they sent me—still a fair way of putting it—to the University of Chicago (again, for only a year). After that, and following a time of about fifteen months, the G.I. Bill sent me back to the university. In the meantime my list of temporary homes had lengthened: Parris Island, South Carolina; Camp Lejeune, North Carolina; Hawaii; Council Bluffs. And there was an overseas intervention between Hawaii and Council Bluffs: fifteen days on a grim, grey island several hundred miles south of Japan... Iwo Jima. I was evacuated from Iwo and spent the next two years recovering from my experience there.

Since then, since my year at the University of Cambridge—to which the University of Chicago had some sort of link in those days—I have lived mainly in the suburbs of Boston, Washington, and Los Angeles, attending to the business of the company I founded and for some years, until I sold it in August 1987, had served as its principal executive.

Between times I began to spend long stretches (the word is apt) on the High Plains of our country, drawn to them irresistibly for reasons that no end of explanation can satisfy. For a time, after I had left the hospital, but before I went back to Dr. Hutchins's university, I used to drive down to Springfield, then head west, across Missouri and into Kansas along U.S. 36, all the car windows rolled down, the road ahead endless, empty, and straight as a die, gliding along for five or six hours until I felt myself slipping away from a world that (no doubt) I connected with huge obligations and demands for which I had no stomach, not excluding the expectations of my mother and a strange dread at the thought of returning to college. There was a certain place, north of Hays, Kansas, where, suddenly, I could look around and see an earth as remote from Decatur and Council Bluffs as it was from anything I would imagine: a vast, spare, treeless, brown land. Conceivably I connected them, these Great Plains, with a purity of possibility, with a certain innocence of expectation (I had never seen a whiteout or a tornado in those days). And the people I began to know in the summers (who never asked where I was from, or what did I "do," or where I had "been to" college) seemed to me to represent certain virtues and simplicities, allegiances to plots of earth, to family, to community—they were clear-eyed, silent, imperturbable, self-reliant. Their plains seemed a giant sweep of independence and clarity.

In 1958 I bought land near Douglas, Wyoming. I have twice added to my original holding. There is some high ground in the foothills of the Laramies; and from the porch of the house I built I can make out the dusty silver trace of the North Platte, and a thin haze, sienna-gold, that settles over the Sand Hills, far to the east, at dusk in summertime. I don't see many people, but there are certain things to love among those native to this soil, qualities their most eloquent celebrant, Gretel Erlich, has perfectly captured: a good-naturedness, she calls it, "that is concomitant with severity, and lives lived in vigor, self-reliance, common sense... in which an [individual] life is not a series of dramatic events for which he or she is applauded, but a slow accumulation of days, seasons, years, anchored by a land-bound sense of place."

All this by way of personal prolegomenon, Robert: why the site is to be here, in what the map tells you is east central Wyoming. I own the land that the venture requires, and I want the students out there.

The Site

Our College will have its being in the clear, windy spacious-
ness of eastern Wyoming, midway between the northeastern
frontage of the Laramies and Thunder Basin, the latter an unre-
lievedly empty grassland, seemingly limitless both to the eye
and, in its blown distances, to the traveller from the North.
Access to our demesne will not be especially easy.

Rugged hills, largely unclothed, shoulder down from the
Laramies, their ridges and ridgelines splayed, many-fingered,
rocky, curled, and taut, grasping the flat shortgrass prairie
directly to our east. We will build the College both on the facing flanks of two ridges that run generally parallel to each other,
and on the valley—a mile wide at the place I have in mind—
that separates them.

I want the Forum sited on this flat grassland. Here the College will conduct much of its ordinary business, in the buildings
(constructed of native materials) prepared for the various necessary functions: classrooms, a library, a dispensary, athletic and
fine arts facilities, and so on. On the adjoining flanks we will
construct four villages, in which mentors and pupils, and a few
of our professors, will live—houses, refectories, guest quarters,
and the like. Such is the nature of the terrain hereabouts—
jagged cross-hatchings of streambeds, empty draws, patches of
conifer, wild rummages of detached meadow, hummocky eminences that never settled into prairie—such is its bulk and its
conformation, that we may site the villages so that they will
not see one another, even at the most barren times of year, and
even though they are but a mile or two apart. Rude roads and
trails will link them with each other, and with the Forum itself.
At the eastern limit of the valley, a ragged arc punctuated by a
few willows and cottonwoods, lies the streambed of the Shel-

drake. This is generously described as a tributary of the North Platte, four miles north of our site. And this, I should say, is important to our purpose, for it was directly along the Platte that both Oregon and Mormon pioneers, their "stern impassioned stress," made their way west, one hundred fifty years ago, following an instinct in some ways linked to our own. There are still a few physical evidences of the trail: a long, grassy swale, visible at the evening limit of the day; a boulder or two; dates and initials cut crudely and perdurable—one set marking a family, I believe, that like mine began its journey from Decatur.

And at the upper jointure of the ridgelines, three miles from the Forum, a robust promontory thrusts itself forward, from which a visitor can look down at all the demesne—some forty-five hundred acres—and beyond it, beyond the silvery trace of the Platte, the unending emptiness of the High Plains, east as far as Nebraska. I want the College chapel built on this promontory. There is a place precisely suitable. I have an image in my mind, not so much of its site as of its interior: all the community is standing together, all facing choir and pulpit, and beyond them a window, hugely panoramic, frames a vista of the Laramies, the Great Plains, and between them the river.

[I have seen the promontory. I have walked to the top, not an easy distance. Adams stretches the vista to provide it a westward prospect; the view, however, is actually more northwest by west. But we will accommodate him so far as we can. The architect is game, but says the soil is friable and stony. R.P.]

The site for the whole College might be imagined as the lower half of the inside of a cone, its lip the Sheldrake. Now imagine that you are at this lip, and walking west, away from the river. Envisage around you for the first four or five minutes of your walk the low, unpretentious structures of the Forum—the academic and other buildings where much of our work will one day be carried on. You ascend imperceptibly, very gradually, the land on either side of you curling upwards gently, ragged fleeces of trees—Russian Olives, aspens, alders—thickening as they climb the hillsides, merging finally in deciduous forest about halfway up the slopes. Your path, as you walk west, meanders in a poky way along an empty streambed; but at distances of about a mile and a half, and then at three miles, marked paths extend outward from your path—outward, more or less at right angles to your direction.

(At l'Ecole Polytechnique in Palaiseau all the streets, avenues, connecting paths, and so on, are quietly named for French heroes of science, government, and military service. Surely we should do this. These are to be quiet signs but fit commemorations of Americans. Those honored will not necessarily be famous Americans, but rather men and women who did things that have proved to be of enduring importance, but whom history has passed by.)

Each path leads to the sites of what will be our College villages—each of them is to be about a mile and a half from the central path. Each will be hidden from the sight of anyone making his way along the path. This is important, as the villages are to be quite separate from one another, and quite distinct, evolving in their own way.

This is a useful place to describe them. As a College community of 1,200—an average student residential census—we will be too large to engender the kind of community, of dailiness, of shared obligation in work and recreation, that I have in mind. We want our students living—we have used the phrase before—in little platoons, not large battalions. A village (an approximation in an eastern university, for size anyway, would be a "quad") provides the intimacy required for our purpose, intimacy of the kind that is the distillate of *communitas*: close gatherings of people devoted to a common purpose, their successes or satisfactions functions of the constancy with which they serve each other's needs, and are able to rely on one another unconsciously. Obviously the College will foster a strong pride, an élan, a prized distinctiveness built of many components: isolation, natural situation, commitment to a unique way of living and learning, and the hardships and demands of its climate. But the villages will provide a different inflection, rather like that of the Benedictine communities that have their being on the Great Plains, that attend to all their own needs, and whose satisfactions inhere largely in serving God through the ways they serve each other.

Each village is to have six "houses," and each house is to serve as residence for about fifty students and three or four mentors. Of the latter I will have much more to say as we proceed; but for now let me identify them only as younger members of the faculty, most of them unmarried, whose collateral responsibilities include serving in the houses and offering tutorial tuition, counseling, and simply the friendship of older persons. (College students today, you know, are never around adults outside of class, because today's professors don't think in terms of leading and serving young students.)

At the center of each house is to be a professor and his family. This person will be one of the few whose residence in the house is to be of long tenure, so that those appointed to the position and to the work must be selected most carefully.

Each student should have his own room—a "single"—and each room should be so sited so as to receive a warm share of the day's sun, and from a large window so placed as to afford the dreaming space all our pupils should be afforded. I see the rooms as simple, austerely comfortable, sparely furnished, their occupants sharing common facilities; the rooms all on-line, all with large worktables and bookshelves.

And of course each house is to have its own living rooms, studies, family rooms, kitchens, libraries.

There are to be no televisions in the common areas of the houses, and none in student rooms; the refectories in the villages will have television, but I want them kept out of the houses—for all the obvious reasons.

Like the buildings in the Forum, I will expect that our houses be designed and planned to make the best, most functional building use of materials as far as possible native to the land hereabouts; and that they *fit* as functionally as possible into the circumstances of their sites. All of the buildings shall be "right" for the region—weathery and strong, warm and spare. We will use as much wood as possible, and buildings are not to be "dramatic." If they ever appear in architectural self-adulatory magazines, we will have failed. There are to be six such houses on each village site, typically no more than a quarter-mile from one another, and generally equidistant from the central structure in each village, the refectory.

Here students and mentors, and the professors on the village sites, will gather twice daily without exception for the breakfast and evening meals.

The Village Refectories

Or, if the word strikes you as outworn and effete, the *village dining halls*. At a point central to the six houses in each of our four villages will lie the real center of each community, the refectory. We will demand that our students and their mentors take their meals in common, sitting at long tables properly laid for each meal, fed on wholesome and simple fare, and, from time to time, asked to listen to certain readings or musical selections, all rendered live. I should add that virtually all the preparation of these meals, including service and clean-up, is to be the work of students and mentors themselves.

Our culture celebrates the harried perkiness of the active professional woman and her sleepy husband, bolting breakfast meals of popped-up carbohydrates as they clatter from the kitchen to the driveway. No children appear in the advertisements for the "product" to be eaten at these furtive times. When the children do appear much later in the day only one parent, or none, is around. The expectation that a family or a group of friends might sit quietly at home together for a meal has vanished. This is why, it seems to me, we must insist that our village communities come together twice a day for meals, for fellowship, for learning, for pleasure. I think, also, that students should be asked to change their places every couple of weeks.

A blessing should be asked at all meals, one suitable to the religious provenances of most of our students. Evening meals, several times a week, should be the occasions for readings by students from classics of American history, written to engage the heart as well as educate the brain. Meals will also furnish useful occasions for debate on assorted issues of contemporary political interest, and all should be required to prepare for and engage in such debates at least twice a year. The College must lose no opportunity to assure that its students know how to eat properly, how to behave in company, how to use their utensils, and so forth. In the early years of the College we will have to insist that professors join refectory meals (most, I should hope, would want to in any case), if only because our mentors will themselves have been raised in the 1970s and 1980s, when no one was taught manners, and when the simple wish that young people *could* be taught manners, expressed anywhere outside an Episcopalian vestry gathering, excited an incredulous ridicule by the young, which assured the craven acquiescence of their elders.

It is good for the community to pause together in this way, each day; for all to enjoy each other's company, and *not*, perhaps, to shine in use. It is even good, from time to time, for us to be bored together. It is often at such times, as the Benedictines say, that the ear of the heart listens most ardently.

The College Calendar

When we ask "How Should They Live?" we must consider how the College organizes its time, and our pupils' time, for the recurrent sequences of College missions and duties. New cohorts appear and graduates depart. We will look closely at the academic uses of the calendar when I describe the academic curriculum later.

I suggest a rather conventional calendar. A student's *cursus* is configured for five years, of which he is to be away from the demesne for about two years altogether. There are to be two long terms annually, each of fourteen weeks, one beginning around September 1, the other March 1; and each long term (allowing for modest vacations) is to be followed by interim periods of six weeks. July should be a vacation month, August a time of orientation for entering and other cohorts, and for a variety of other activities to be described later, for continuing classes.

In the last long term of a student's tenure, in Year V, we might require some capstone, individual academic enterprise, one culminating in a proposal to address an issue of current national importance, and which will draw from the stock of experiences—intellectual and practical—a student will have accumulated at the College. In the other long terms, most will enroll in five academic courses. (For a while I considered having all students do only one academic course for a period of several weeks—the "bloc system"—but it is not right for us, remembering that Cohort I comprises three hundred new students, very young, many of them not so well prepared as we would like; I am afraid that they must be plunged into several courses immediately.)

During the six-week interims students will study one subject alone, typically one of their two required languages. The interim nearest their overseas residence will always be given to a study of the language spoken in the country to which they will be sent. Two of the interims will be spent on public service, the students assigned randomly to a variety of duties, all over the United States, in positions of the kind considered menial. For example, as assistants in Emergency Admissions facilities in large hospitals; as teaching assistants in the most deprived of our schools; as attendants in nursing homes. I must insist on this. It is in these works that our cleverest undergraduates are likely to learn something about who *they* are and what they should be educating themselves for. Our "eliteness" inheres partly in instilling a permanent sense of obligation in those who need what we, by virtue of good fortune, are being educated to provide. These "internships" by our students will be less "Lest We Forgets" than periods of time in which we may test ourselves in what we are learning, or rather in what we are preparing ourselves for; so much of which, over long careers of service, must be by way of helping those who, for whatever reason, cannot look out for themselves.

I noted the use of interims for the study of languages. During the first long term of the third year, members of Cohort III will be abroad—in the Middle or Far East, in Africa, India, Indonesia, or Russia, attaining a required fluency in a non-Western language. Such fluency will be a prerequisite for completion of our curriculum; and not only attaining linguistic proficiency strong enough that it can sustain itself for many years, but also learning the history, culture, political and economic circumstances, and current conditions of the countries to which they are assigned. Such required deployments seem almost self-evidently necessary for a college with our mission and at our time in American history.

To return to the calendar: first, those away during the mid-winter interims, those that follow the Christmas holiday, will be spared one or two Wyoming winters, or at least their most punishing depths. Hereabouts in these months the hills are a grey-blown frigidity, the cold stunning and fathomless, the wind a hoarse, unceasing ovation—like the sound of a gigantic throng in a football stadium. At the College it will be an annual time of hunkering down against such perils and punishments. But it will be a time also in which the community—houses, villages, the College itself—in feeding upon its own resources, will find new ones, deeper ones, in the brotherhood, the sense of *communitas* and family, thus engendered. For which, even in bleakest February, we may feel ourselves grateful.

Few human communities are as fully and delicately interfused, in all their elements and textural lineaments, as small colleges. They hallow in mission and structure the gifts of forbearers at the turn of another millennium. But among colleges still living, it is difficult to conceive any in which the successful execution of a stated mission is more fully dependent on the character of its *communitas*, on the way the parts cohere, how the crook-taloned birds consort together, than what our College community must be, if it is to succeed.

Living at the College

All Americans who have worn their country's uniform, or who have passed through the rites of passage common to its nurseries of training, imagine they remember a fearsome authority figure who told them, by way of welcome, "Look to the left of you, look to the right of you. One of those people won't be there when this program ends!" The psychology is dubious, as dubious as the memory that has fixed and heightened the scene.

For the message should surely be this: "Look to the left of you, look to the right, and make this resolve: your mission is to help your brother (or sister) through this program!" Such an opening salvo is formidable enough, but its burden, still heavy, is radically different. Were it to be embodied in a manual of some sort, we might call it *Looking Out for #2*. Every aspect of the way our students are to live at the College must be anchored in, must pivot about, a willing commitment to do their duty to the community, to their colleagues and friends before they attend to their own needs or wishes. Living according to this *ethos* will be one of our means of preparing graduates to be virtuous and disinterested citizens—and leaders. The notion of community is essential to our purpose. The College's community must be inflected at all points by this paramount obligation: to members of Trek teams, houses, villages, cohorts, to the College. To put it in terms that may still be familiar to military trainees: the winning unit is the one whose *last* member crosses the finish line before the last member of all competing units.

All aspects of College life are to be organized around an *ethos* of responsibility rather than of privilege, of duty rather than impulse, of need rather than want. Can there be anything more useful to the education of the generation that will be first to enroll—a generation completely self-absorbed, all its wants catered to by an avid commercial *apparat* and by the absence of interested or competent parental supervision?

I intend that the way our students live both affirm and demonstrate our allegiance to this, implementing culture. Our currency of success is to be an unusual, fructifying admixture of mother wit, tenacity of purpose, and generosity of spirit and mind. Students are to be judged less by what they do than by what they *are*. And at the beginning of their *cursus*, no student is to have any advantage over another, aside from those given by Nature's God, or by the happy circumstances of earlier education or family. If men and women are to be judged by the content of their character, as Dr. King hoped we might be, our College community must be firm in its adherence to usages that educate (and train) students to such a desideratum.

Sumptuary Requirements, Disciplinary Expectations

Students at the College are not to have money. They will not be allowed motor vehicles. They are not to adorn their persons with vanities of tonsure, or clothing that draws attention either to itself or to its wearer. They are to maintain in their rooms only those appliances common to all—laptops, certainly, CD players, and the like. On the other hand, they are encouraged to accumulate books and paintings, and they should learn how to husband their resources carefully in order to indulge themselves in these ways. We will encourage frequent showings of paintings, drawings, photographs, and the like, both by visitors and our own pupils; and each of the houses in our villages will maintain guest apartments for such practitioners of the spatial and graphic arts.

But to take these things one at a time.

Certain phrases, however ancient and however often repeated, never become clichés, so vivid and plangent is the force that buoys their words. One of the common concerns money: He wanted to *get his hands on it.*

Americans relish money, far less for what it can "do" than for what it seems to them to be: a means of validating stature and a way of establishing invidious ascendancies over others; or to set themselves apart, money being the enabler, from others. It is the sustaining spring of vapid insolence and contumely: the four thousand pairs of shoes laid up in the closet of a woman who never leaves her house.

I frankly desire the College to inculcate an indifference to it. I understand that as I communicate this wish I expose myself both to the obloquy of hypocrisy and the ridicule of an imputed utopianism. As to the first, I can but asseverate that the acquiring of wealth was never my aim; it was the consequence of my work in the semiconductor business. As to the second, I believe that if the College may demonstrate that a competence can satisfy the needs of a fulfilling life, we shall have done useful service for our pupils. Further, that if we may show that a competence (by which I mean a sufficient income to attend the needs proper to a citizen of the kind we are preparing) may displace, or rather prevent even the conception of, the passion for money, then we may make them exemplary legatees of our curriculum. We may acknowledge with Boswell that "making money is one of the greatest pleasures in life, as it is very lasting and continually increasing. But it must be observed that a great share of anxiety is the constant concomitant of this passion, so that the mind is as much hurt in one way as it is pleased in another."

I set down such reflections much less in the spirit of censure than as a means for the training of those few students enrolled in our College.

The students are not to have money. They should be given an amount of scrip at the beginning of each term necessary to attend to their needs, and this allowance should be reasonable rather than niggardly. For purposes of travel, for assignments abroad, for service internships and vacations, of course we shall provide the necessary currency or credit. As I suggest, their needs at the College will be modest, but they should be liberally, fairly, attended to: not excluding an ample provision for recreations, personal items necessary to health and grooming, clothing, stationery, books, and the like.

"The stern virtue of the patriot" that Abigail Adams studied and cherished in her husband is simply not compatible with an overriding interest in the acquisition of money. Again: should the growth of a fortune, as by-product of some salutary endeavor, be the consequence of that achievement, then— depending on how the fortune is used—we ought not denigrate its owner. Yet the foul wake that nowadays churns along behind its acquisition, seeming to pollute and infect more than it vivifies and cleanses, appears ineluctably toxic when it touches political men and matters.

I want our graduates, in short, to live indifferent to its acquirement; their talents must be consecrated to other purposes.

As to automobiles and the like, if students own them, they should be allowed to bring them to some place, not less than ten miles from the demesne, where they may remain until the beginning of any authorized absences from the College. We should provide end and beginning of term transport, of course, from the airports and bus terminals nearest the demesne. I intend that the College itself be self-sufficient as to the resources needed to sustain not only all our pupils' instruction inside and out-of-doors, but also their recreations.

As I say, clothing should be severely functional. Here we should not prescribe too closely. Obviously warm outer-garments will be a requirement, clothing of the kind worn on the great Wyoming sheep and cattle spreads. For College chapels, College assemblies, certain meals in the refectories, and annual administrations of the *sacramentum* (about which, more later), dress should be a bit more formal. As to jewelry: a watch and a ring are reasonable and unvain accoutrements.

Again: the old saying that books furnish a room, adapted to the needs of village rooms and the cyberage, seems appropriate still. We need not particularize too finely.

Serving the College Community

Most of those duties that in an ordinary college are relegated to paid, "classified" employees, should, in our College, be assigned to students. I want exempted only certain jobs that require technical expertises that we cannot expect our students to have; and certain managerial billets that need full-time, generally older incumbents. The cost savings will be substantial: think, Robert, in terms of thirty classified employees instead of one hundred.

But that is not what impels my insistence on this point. In my scheme it is necessary that all members of the student community depend on the steady efficiency, reliable and permanent, of the work of their fellows; and that they become used to serving them without compensation—and that a fair part of that service be in work that "educated" Americans normally do not do. Student assignments to the various tasks should be rotated, incidentally, and reasonable attention given the varying burdens and difficulties of each task. Quartered safe out here in the soft dusk of late spring, one can easily forget what winter will demand of everyone on the demesne, not excluding work that must be done out-of-doors. It will be formidable.

The more senior students will lead various teams attending to different chores. Here is another practical school of leading: more sure-footed in what it inculcates than mere classes in "leadership," and far more lasting in the lessons it impresses.

Under no circumstances is "work" to be used for purposes of chastisement or punishment. To borrow from *St. Benedict's Rules for Monasteries*:

> And if the circumstances of the place... should require that they themselves do the work of gathering the harvest, let them not be discontented; for then are they truly monks when they live by the labor of their hands, as did our Fathers.

We might replace the name of monks with the phrase *students of our College*: for ours is but an adaptation, for purposes entirely secular, of this idea. Our clerisy, our American professional class, spurns such work and does not ask its children to perform such labor. Rather it condescends to felicitate the children on their state, each by each, of being "special"—without requiring them to earn the accolade, such as it is, by doing hard work that they may not always like doing.

A Suggested Daily Schedule for the College

Students who elect to study Latin at the College will read Caesar. They will note the brisk and simple felicity of his prose, and the recurrent employment of the grammatical construction known as the Ablative Absolute: These things having been done. The phrase is always followed by: "He next turned his attention to…." Caesar, like Lord Curzon, Harry Truman, and George Marshall, moved smoothly from one task to another, the foregoing sealed as it were hermetically from the next: without emotional baggage or loss of powers of concentration or energy. Such an ability, which we must surely aim to help inculcate, is usually allied to the ability to make sharp, productive use of small periods of time. No prospective citizen or leader of promise should leave the College without such trained abilities.

Though the daily schedule (with amendments for Sabbath observances) should be regularity itself, broad swaths of time within that pattern should be laid open—and given the students to use entirely for their own purposes. They will answer many obligations and masters; yet they must learn on their own to respond to all their conflicting, pressing demands in ways that satisfy them all. Moreover, I insist that they be required to spend some significant portion of that time alone, partly for thinking their own thoughts (rather than reading the thoughts of others), and partly in attending to their duties without worrying about the bustling, visible busy-ness on which contemporary American business puts so absurd a premium—an idiot mania that does nothing but promote dissipating superficialities of activity, like car salesmen on television, affecting to stride excitedly from one vehicle to another.

I suggest the following:

0530	Rising
0600	Breakfast in refectories for students and mentors
0700	Solitary time in the houses or on the demesne
0900	Class, tutorials, lectures, laboratories, seminars

1200	Lunch in refectories or Forum cafeteria (optional)
1300	Afternoon class or study
1500	Trek, athletics, fitness
1800	Supper in refectories
1930	Private study, College activities, meetings

I would not require a "Lights Out," except perhaps for the first-year cohort.

The schedule obviously will be amended for the variety of special activities that occur on a weekly or biweekly basis. "Trek," of which I will have something to say later on, will remove groups of students from the demesne, sometimes with mentors, usually twice per long term.

The schedule allows time for students to get from one village to another, or to the Forum, for various fixtures.

There are to be no class cuts. The provision for solitary time is deliberate, and should be enforced by the mentors assigned each house.

Parietal Arrangements

Each of our four villages will house about three hundred students, members of Cohorts I, II, III, and V (Cohort IV will be away serving the College's required military service). The ordinary population of students will be somewhat less, given various off-demesne activities, terms abroad, or in-service assignments.

As we have seen, those three hundred are divided among six houses, each house with its complement of mentors and, usually, a professor and his family.

The houses will be restricted to members of one sex. Reasonable provision for visitation among members of the different houses should be made.

I am not troubled by the expected criticism that our housing policy, as regards young men and young women, is retrograde or old-fashioned. That something is old does not make it wrong. Thirty years ago, many male high school runners ran the mile in 4:10 or 4:12; now, nearing the turn of the millennium, the best of them do it in 4:15. "New occasions teach new duties, Time makes ancient good uncouth." In fact, time is morally neutral; and for every instance we can provide of time's advance being accompanied by something good, we may adduce another, of something bad. Having college women and men live together in the same dormitories is not proper. Any college that houses unmarried undergraduates of both sexes in the same dormitory communicates implicitly (published regulations notwithstanding) its endorsement of premarital sex. Any dormitory that makes condoms available positively invites sexual relations among its students. What is pertinent is not the message a college thinks it is sending, but the communication the students believe they are hearing.

I may be forgiven an authorial intrusion. The practice of sexual cohabitation, by "hall" or dormitory if not by room or suite, had become general by the early 1970s. Five years later, the studentry, now exhausted and beginning to return to the cultivation of its own gardens rather than the world's, grew quiet and eschewed protest marches and occupations of administrative offices. It cut its hair. Its elders (men and women at this writing now in the springtimes of their senility), grateful for the quiet, left in place everything that the counterculture had caused: most importantly the expectation that the young of both sexes should have unimpeded access, on campuses, to one another, at all times. One forlorn but enervated administrator asked only that his students be safely out of the dormitory of the other sex not later than BMNT: the Beginning of Morning Nautical Twilight. Keep up appearances, don't you know?

Fit for Duty

Just as the American academy has long since abandoned its ancient avowed mission to promote virtue along with good learning, it has either forsworn or forgotten its former expectation that students be held to standards of physical fitness, or raised to them at least. That is putting it too strenuously. There was an expectation, it is better to say, that young men in good colleges would seek physical hardihood, athletic accomplishment, and hearty commitment to outdoor pursuits. Many colleges insisted that students demonstrate competence in swimming, boxing, gymnastics, or other activities of physical culture. For those who did not "go in for" games, the simple character of living promoted general fitness among undergraduates. To read through the journals of nineteenth-century students in Britain and America is to reenter a world in which fifteen-mile walks were matters of routine, in which all lived in dormitories where conditions of living were austere at best.

I think of Gladstone's diary and two entries capturing his life at Oxford:

June 25—*Ethics*. Collections 9–3. Among other things wrote a long paper on religions of Egypt, Persia, Babylon; and on the Satirists. Finished packing books and clothes. Left Oxford between 5–6, and walked fifteen miles towards Leamington. Then obliged to put in, being caught by a thunderstorm. Comfortably off in a country inn at Steeple Aston. Read and spouted some *Prometheus Victus* there.

June 26—Started before 7. Walked eight miles to Banbury. Breakfast there, and walked on twenty-two to Leamington. Arrived there and changed. Gaskell came in the evening. *Life of Massinger.*

This, in some ways, should be our ideal. But today the cultivation of the mind is all that elite universities care for—with the exception of athletic teams that are a form of big business, that bring in money.

We will be different. The College will demand our pupils be fit and prove it, and often. The instrument for attaining that fitness will be a taxing regime—exhilaratingly so—of physical culture. And it would be idle to build our school where we are going to—on a rugged haunch of hill at the edge of the American High Plains, indeed in our country's emptiest state—without using its resources to promote this purpose.

"This purpose" in turn comprises several others, and it is in their service that the first trustees and faculty should prepare for this aspect of our mission:

1. The inculcation of what was once called a positive addiction: to outdoor lives, outdoor recreations and sports, of the kind that both promote hardihood and sustain aerobic and muscular fitness. No student should be graduated who is not addicted to fitness, and to earning and maintaining his fitness outdoors.

2. The demonstration, never to be forgotten, that every student can overcome the most robust challenges to his physical abilities and courage, and to his resolution in the face of long hardship in straitened circumstances.

3. The learning of leading in the most formidable and most permanent way possible: by having to lead, rally, inspire one's own friends during times of physical hardship, great fatigue, and deprivation.

4. The learning of certain technical skills that will be useful later in life: among them the skills of mountaineering, orienteering, swimming, living off the land, parachuting. Scaling the sides of mountains— grossly to oversimplify—leads to an ineradicable confidence in one's ability to function efficiently in circumstances of sustained danger, in which absolute concentration of a prolonged character (like, say, that of an oncologist or a concert virtuoso) is a prerequisite to success and satisfaction both. It taxes many abilities simultaneously, and it provides a most useful training avenue for learning to lead.

5. The habit of comfort and confidence in being alone in remote places, and able to shift for oneself in such circumstances.

6. Learning to judge the terrain, topography, rivers, the mountain West and the High Plains, and the weathers that inflect their climate.

7. Learning a lifetime competitive sport, and learning it to a certain demonstrated plateau of excellence and mastery: a sport that taxes physical abilities as well as mental ones; that provides ready surcease from the clamant obligations of work (those things now called "stress"); but that does not, commonly, attract overwrought and undue attentions to itself.

8. Learning to live and work efficiently in times and circumstances of pain or danger, and to ignore their solicitations.

9. Learning to function competently, productively, and usefully as a member of a team.
10. Learning the arts of self-defense, hunting, and fishing.

I do not wish to specify unduly, to "micromanage"; but I may perhaps be allowed a few more observations and suggestions.

First, I *do* intend to make provision in my estate for a fully equipped gymnasium, with all the facilities necessary to sustain a comprehensive program of physical fitness and ordinary athletic pursuits. Calculate the money that the estate will *not* be providing for the construction of a stadium: that will not be inconsiderable; the sum should be able to provide extraordinary facilities—and in the long Wyoming winters most will be used and used constantly.

Second, I see few opportunities for competitive athletics between the College and other colleges or universities in the state or nearby. We neither "match up well" nor present a calendar that would enable regular competition on a regular footing. Obviously the College would not permit women or men on a team to miss a scheduled seminar or tutorial, or other prescribed activity on the demesne, in order to compete. Nor of course will we countenance the recruitment of pupils whose *main* demonstration of aptitude and attractiveness has been athletic.

Third, let me describe several of the athletic/fitness enterprises and tests that I think the College should insist upon:

1. *Trek:* "Trek" will put down deep roots quickly. Our students will embrace both the concept and the activity itself. In the opening orientation month, members of Cohort I would be taught the rudiments of "living in the field," and of survival theory (principles of relevant tools, orienteering, physiology,

first aid, living in and off nature, field garments and cover, and so on). I would send them out in teams of three or four, on easy acclimatization missions in the wilderness. Later, much longer Treks might vary the team numbers, include some solitary missions, and increase elements of risk. I envisage a standard "issue," depending on the time of year, for all College Trekkers, i.e., waterproof sheet, one book of matches, one minimum sustenance ration, one length of nylon rappel rope and carabiners, windbreaker, and so on. Again: this may be varied. Trek is a tremendous leadership laboratory, especially when membership in teams is randomly assigned, and when Trekkers must handle conditions of great fatigue, heat, or cold. As proficiency increases, so can the nature of team challenges—for example: requiring teams to move certain heavy objects over long distances; to surmount natural obstacles; to learn how to cross swift rivers. The country hereabouts is unmatched for this activity. It is certain that our graduates, veterans of perhaps as many as twenty Treks during their tenure at the College, will leave us capable of surviving, and surviving confidently, in virtually any circumstance—and indeed *craving* opportunities to continue such adventures through their lives. For there is something to the argument that, having been through experiences that do search out our abilities to survive in extended periods of alien or unpleasant challenges, we grow in confidence. Equally there is no better or more natural way to sustain the hardihood which, I believe, is an important objective of our form of education.

I would always allow Trekkers to carry journals. But no books.

For several days twice during the August orientation session, and thereafter twice a term, three- to seven-person teams should be given a destination, within fifty miles of the demesne, and told to be there by a certain time and date. Teams should be furnished minimal provisions and equipments necessary to make their Treks likely successes, if all perform as they should. Obviously the nature of the terrain to be negotiated, obstacles to be surmounted, and timing of the various missions will dictate the length of time allotted to each Trek.

Assignments to teams should be entirely random, but with representation from all cohorts. This "spontaneous teaming," as Mr. Brinkman at Bell Labs calls a parallel practice in physical-sciences research, unites in useful synergy a variety of talents and skills—and, probably, liabilities.

It may sound bland, but a survey of the land within a radius of fifty miles of the College will show that the implications of Treks are anything but bland. They—and Treks undertaken from sites farther afield, but still in Wyoming—will tax and test and reward many skills and qualities of character, of leading, of friendship. Leading friends of one's own generation is a matchless crucible for learning to lead.

From time to time, Treks will be designated as *Solitaries*.

Contemporary technology readily supports an efficient system of locating and communicating with Trek teams, and of monitoring their progress.

2. *The Marathon or the Triathlon:* All second- and fifth-year students should train for and complete the full distance of a marathon (to be run on the demesne or nearby); or a regular triathlon, whose aggregate distance is not less than fifty miles.

3. *Boxing:* I am determined that boxing be required in the fitness/athletics program. In my mind a fundamental purpose of

boxing is conjoined with that of our requirement that every student master a non-Western language, and live in the country for a term where that language is spoken: both experiences lodge deeply in the student the predisposition to assess, always to work to understand, the nature and character of other men and women, other cultures, other countries. Americans are terrible at this, by temperament and by provenance. Abroad, they think that if they are "nice," or generous, or aw-shucks stumbly, then their hosts will like them. At home, so intent are we upon our own concerns that we do not—as a matter of course—consider the implications for others of our own avid commitments or endeavors.

Boxing inculcates the lifelong habit of studying one's adversary, one's fellow competitor. It promotes a healthy wariness, the habit of assessment, of objectively making inventory of an adversary's weak points, strengths, skills, character, motivation, fitness. Beware of entrance to a quarrel, but being in, bear't that the opposed may beware of *thee*.

Besides these things, and far more pertinent: here is a sport, boxing, in which a competitor must make a conscious decision to put himself at risk; in which success pitilessly demands the sustained cooperative performance by several aspects of personal fitness, character, and strength. No one who has tried to box for a round or two, and who is neither conditioned nor skilled in the sport, will forget how desperately overmatched *in every way* he felt himself, after only thirty seconds. And to repeat: in no sport is it more consequential that a cold intelligence superintend performance, even as instinct, training, and preparation work to hone an aggressive temperament, and to attain the desired success.

4. The learning and mastery of skills and equipment needed for survival: To this I need add little, besides noting that it will be important for faculty to hire mentors who will be accomplished survivalists, or graduates of such training and experience (such as retired special forces officers or noncommissioned officers) who can teach these skills and explain their importance.

We are a soft country, a country of spectators, of passive receptors of stimulations that keep us inert or provide senseless *longueurs* between periods of work. Our universities are indifferent to the provision of serious remedies for the phenomenon. Most of the American clerisy, particularly those who take seriously their roles and status as those who profess an academic discipline, either have never trained their bodies to serve the concomitant needs of their minds and characters, or, out of an aversion to physical exercise or sports in youth, have cultivated an ignorant condescension to fitness, strength, athletic excellence, and to the skills of survival, or of confident living out-of-doors. To see them, fat and grey, dismounting from their utility vehicles or campers, during fretful family visits to our national parks (the air-conditioned campers filled with portable TVs, washing machines, faxes, and the rest), is to see what too many of us Americans have allowed a century of material abundance to do to us.

Yet I ache to communicate something else: my own love for our land, most especially for the mountains and the plains of the West, and for the pleasures, ineffable, triumphant, unceasing, that they provide us always—should we go often to earn them, on their terms, not ours, and should we undertake, as among our most sacred obligations as citizens, our duties to sustain and protect them.

A Responsible Community: Honor Embodied at the College

In the most virtuous and rigorous of our colleges, "Honor" is used most often as the first word of a phrase: Honor Code. Typically such an honor code proscribes certain forms of conduct, and it prescribes severe punishments for breaches of the code. Several colleges maintain, still, what is called the "single sanction": if you are found guilty of a breach of the code, you will be dismissed.

I am in sympathy with these codes. Their aim, transparent enough, is to mark a student's conscience and character for life; to mark it with an alert, positive revulsion toward the forms of conduct the codes forbid—typically, lying, cheating, stealing. Some enjoin an obligation to report breaches of their codes, either to an administrative or student tribunal, and to penalize those who, while having knowledge of an offense against the code, fail to report the transgression or transgressors.

Our first trustees, mentors, professors, and students must consider the question of honor during the first months and years of the College's life, and consider it with particular reference to the College's mission. No doubt they will remind themselves that the code (or whatever they decide to call it) is being prepared for a generation of high school students, now joining the College, who have attended schools where the majority are persistent and industrious cheaters; or, if they are not themselves cheaters, are young persons unlikely under any circumstances to "report" on their friends. A smaller percentage are thieves. The reasons for their cheating and thieving are close at hand, and obvious: they either passively or actively emulate adults, or they live in a school environment in which successful cheating gains palpable advantages, in which the climate of toleration is powerful, and in which punishments, if given, are absurdly mild, such as writing an "ethical essay," or apologizing to someone, or being suspended for a day or two.

I do not insist on the word "code," because I have in mind something larger and more comprehensive for our students—an understanding of virtue and honor that is nowhere near so bitten down, so limited in its expectations of good conduct, as merely to insist that students will not "lie, steal or cheat, or tolerate those who do." Yes, such strictures should be included, but we should also demonstrate not only that such actions are proscribed but also that they lead, literally, to nothing useful, appealing, or worthy. In this, we will be unlike contemporary American society, where those who have achieved celebrity or their Warholian fifteen minutes of fame are routinely caught in acts of dishonor. Their rehabilitation is immediate, their sins trumpeted as endearing or leavening eccentricities, and their invitation to appear on "talk" shows or to write articles assured. A routine concomitant of the process of Being Caught and Being Rehabilitated is seeking "help," *viz*, "he should get counseling" of the kind that will "bring closure" and help him "put the matter behind him." We will expose and not tolerate this kind of mealy-mouthed immorality.

We should note, too, that if the proscribed trinity of lying, stealing, and cheating (and its common contemporary component, plagiarizing) is placed on a raised pedestal of obloquy, with special punishments reserved for their commission, most students will infer that other forms of conduct that we would call unvirtuous or dishonorable are… well, not that bad— because I didn't actually cheat or lie about it.

Again: I am not concerned with whether the culture into which we will send our graduates is corrupt, and whether dishonorable behavior continues to advance men and women in the culture. My concern is rather with forging so strong an allegiance to principles of honorable conduct by our students that (1) they will not be attracted to the prospective advantages, such as they are, of cheating or lying or stealing, and (2) they will not be willing to commit such acts even if they are, for some reason, attracted to the rewards they might confer. If a man scorns the laying up for himself a treasure on earth, as offering no good use to him (if he is content with Aristotle's moderate and sufficient property), he will not be inclined to steal. If he understands that lying is reprehensible, that he must tell the truth at all times, or say nothing, and that lies bring him no advantage but corrode the steel of his soul, he will not be inclined to lie. And if the only advantage that may accrue by cheating, in whatever form, is illusory, he will not be likely to cheat. Above all, for I remain without illusion about the dark recesses of human nature, all human nature, our training at the College ought to be such that, at the very least, Conscience will be clamant—sensitive, loud, and insistent—when the "opportunity" to commit such actions is presented.

No academic advantage can accrue, at our College, to the cheater. There are three associated reasons. First, there is to be no such thing as academic standing relative to other pupils, and no "grades" as they are understood by most schools and colleges. Tutors and mentors will measure understanding of subjects undertaken, and measure such understanding with great care, but they will not "give grades," nor will students pursue them.

Second: the way understanding is measured will itself demonstrate plainly that there is no advantage to cheating, even if it were possible. Supposing in one of our orientation courses that a student has to dismantle, then reconfigure in a prescribed way, the engine of a Jeep? And supposing the success of the test depended only on the Jeep's performance immediately after the exercise—in, say, a twenty-five–mile road test? How could a student cheat, and where would it get him? He would have no idea that this test was going to involve the Jeep, as opposed to, say, an old Ford or a Chevy pick-up—because he would not be assigned "his" vehicle until a moment before the "test." Or, to use a more common example, supposing her work in the history of the Roman Republic (a requirement, incidentally, for all students) demanded the preparation of an essay, of eight or ten pages, every three weeks, the essay to be read aloud before a mentor or professor, one who knew the student well. Understanding in such venues cannot be counterfeited; and the lack of understanding, given the nature of our community and its purposes, could not be tolerated by the student any more than her mentor will tolerate it.

Third: the students live in their houses and villages, serving together in them and in their refectories, and in hundreds of other ways that establish a daily interdependence, an intimacy of sharing and of a need for common understanding and mutual accommodation that will transcend normal human antipathies and petty grievances—in such an atmosphere it is not likely that individual students will be motivated to act dishonorably.

I would suggest certain usages, in any case, to communicate the College's commitment to the principles enunciated.

There should indeed be a binding *sacramentum*, an oath, taken at the time of enrollment, in August of the student's beginning of his *cursus*, an oath not to the College but to his fellow students, to students at the College past and present—an oath in which he promises not to break faith with them, just as he expects they have not, and will not, break faith with him. The principles of conduct they embrace, they embrace in common.

Second: the program of honor (or whatever it will be called) must be led and administered entirely by students at the College—not by presidents, professors, or mentors. It should be made known, widely and in detail, to all entering students, and there should be regular discussions of its provisions and its means of implementation in the refectories, classes, and chapel.

Third: I insist that a feature of our honor system be confrontation—direct, personal confrontation at the time of the commission of the suspected offense, if it has been witnessed. To me this is preferable to "turning him in" (invidiously, it is whispered, behind his back), for two reasons: (1) because it provides the person suspected of the offense a chance to offer an explanation immediately, and indeed the offense may be innocent; (2) the act of confrontation, searchingly difficult for American adolescents, must be carried out as a duty, and the commission of that duty inculcates a measure of confidence, of the sort that each succeeding act of moral courage instills in young people. It is from hundreds of these small difficult acts that an active lifetime of integrity is derived and strengthened beyond consciousness of itself.

Ours is certainly not to be a climate of moral vigilance, in which all search for moral flaws in everyone else. To the contrary, the sense of *communitas* that fuses our pupils in common aims, hardships, pleasures, and duties will make such confrontations rare.

Beyond this—supposing that the confronter *has* in fact caught a student in the act of stealing—my view is that he should instruct the thief (1) to make immediate restitution, (2) to apologize to the person or agency from whom the object was stolen, and (3) to report himself to a student committee, tribunal, or court. In the early days of the life of the College, fit punishments must be determined for such offenses, and in my judgment they should be severe and exemplary. I do not believe that certain forms of intellectual penitence are appropriate substitutes for punishment of offenses against our honor regulations. I have in mind requiring students to write long essays exploring moral themes, or the views on such issues of Plato, Kant, Mill, or the like of that. Understanding such things has alas little to do with the likelihood that we will or will not act on that understanding in the future.

A Note on Student Discipline and Punishment

What is the purpose of discipline in a residential college? Clearly it is to aid the college in the fulfillment of its mission. It is to help imbue students with convictions about what constitutes proper and honorable behavior; and, so far as possible, with the habits that such convictions, if lived, may become. Self-command is learned best in a community that extols and rewards virtuous behavior, and that demonstrates the efficacy of honorable behavior.

"Punishment" should chastise, yes; but it must also be a positive means by which an undergraduate offender can learn something *useful* from that punishment. It is important that our College not employ as "punishment" certain assignments of community service work, or work that citizens of our community are asked to undertake anyway. Discipline and punishment should be provident and regular (I quote Tocqueville) but not minute. The College should treat students as fully fledged adult members of the community, and not impose many restrictions on their conduct.

Certain breaches of discipline, however, are not to be tolerated. I expect that anyone who brings illegal drugs onto the demesne, for the purpose of distribution or sale to others, be dismissed from the College. Any use of illegal drugs should also be cause for dismissal. The use of alcohol is to be prohibited also.

Americans at the end of the twentieth century have become great ones for suggesting that offenders need "help," and that they should be given recurrent opportunities to rehabilitate themselves. Most offenders of the kind I have in mind do not need help; they need character—just as men and women who are hard put to end their habit of smoking cigarettes do not need nicotine patches; they too need character. Similarly, the idea of rehabilitating student cheaters by having them enroll in classes on "ethics" and write papers on "Why Cheating Is Bad," and the like, is ridiculous.

Of less momentous importance: the College should insist that all students meet all their class, meal, tutorial, and Trek obligations, on time and without exception. No "cuts" are to be permitted.

Solitude

Not so many years ago, in the time of Kennedy, it was supposed that Man would soon be troubled by excessive leisure, and that the advent of yet more sophisticated machines would so reduce the need for his own productive work that he might do as he pleased for most of his days. A common image of that time was one of parties of men and women travelling in a car (which glided to its destination without human direction), playing cards, and in untroubled conversation; and wearing tennis clothes. The abundant sunniness of life without (what we now call) stress lay before us all like a lovely spring meadow, limitless, caressed by the gentle zephyrs of perpetual warmth. No steep and sided hail impended. No clinging reminder that, as Wallace Stevens wrote, "the imperfect is our paradise."

The opposite has happened. The diagnosis is shared so broadly that nothing need be said. The country that nears what is called, with wearisome reiteration, the beginning of the millennium (one, Robert, I shall never see) is a country of manic, feverish, vehement labor and of insensate business connectedness, hostile in every usage to our need for silence and solitude, even the silence and solitude that must be an artificial, unnatural graft, daily interventions spatchcocked into lives choked by a million obligations, signifying... but let it pass. What Froude called that "silent, dreamy vacancy, in which the mind ruminates or rests folded up within itself in the consciousness of its own immortality," cannot and does not subsist in the daily curriculum of *fin de siècle* America. And I remember, if the authorial intrusion may be forgiven, a small sermon preached on Iwo Jima in 1945, after we had secured the island, and its text: *The wind blows where it will and you hear the sound of it, but you do not know whence it comes or whither it goes.* I wonder whether its incongruity is larger now than it was then, in the desperate silence that follows the most savage and calamitous battles, or in the silence a man knows when he walks into an empty house after burying his wife.

Therefore build into the daily curriculum—I have shown where you might put it—an hour of silence and contemplation, a time in which we ordain and expect all our students will allow themselves to be alone with whatever their souls and minds set before them. I insist that this daily hour be something lodged so deeply, as habit and expectation, that they will as a matter of conscience always find ways to sustain it for the rest of their lives, however and wherever they may live, however and whatever clamant industry may intrude upon it.

And so, Robert, you might say we are performing an intervention. The lives of our students are going to be profoundly different from the lives they are leaving behind them. But those we propose to educate and to train, those whose lives we propose to alter, are not alcoholics. Ours is a different kind of intervention. They, especially those in our first cohorts, are the tribunes of a strange, straggling little American generation. The circumstances of their lives would seem to be hostile to everything we believe. If we profess that we "more than self our country love," they have been raised in a country that to them is a notion only, to which they sense or pledge no obligation. If we yet revere heroes and believe in a salutary emulation of their characters and lives, they seem to venerate only those who live the excesses we abominate. If we live lives dictated by the usages of reason and moral obligation, they inhabit a culture that mistrusts reason almost entirely, confounds it with task-oriented information-gathering, and acknowledges the moral obligation only of acquiescence in the claims of friendship. If we live lives of settled resistance to the solicitations of impulse, they indulge lives of acquiescence in all impulses, lives in which all wants are easily gratified, in which the only currency of purchase is "I want." The secular priestesses of this culture are those denominated as soccer moms—adult enablers whose own lives pivot on driving them to malls, games, parties, classes, oases of every description where the "I wants" may be gratified immediately.

These apples are piled up around huge orchards: their parents' own generation. For our first cohorts will be the children of parents who themselves came of age in that time of moral exhaustion, the American 1970s. I alluded to it earlier in these notes, to the spiritual desolation that followed a time of bright idealism smashed and disillusioned. We had gone to Vietnam to save it from communists; we had obeyed the moral imperatives of heartsick consciences on matters of race. We failed in both. The parents of our first cohorts, twenty-five or thirty in 1970 or 1975, were by then passive cynics themselves—empty volcanoes. Within ten years all they could think or say was said better for them in the jingle of a beer commercial: "Who says you can't have it all?" This generation had become, in the memorable phrase of a great writer, the story of a stomach. Our first cohorts have been raised (this is surely the wrong word) by them. These youngsters seem to want what *they* have, only earlier in life; in larger abundance, without working very hard for it, without stopping to examine what the "it" is, and with a passive, resentful acquiescence in their failure to gain, have, or own it. Admittedly, numbers of our first students will be refugees from their own generation, refugees of one sort or another— and this will help. On the whole, however, we will be working to educate a generation at the beginning that does not really know what it wants.

By far the strongest element in this intervention is the communitarian life we are prescribing. St. Benedict established a school for the service of the Lord; we, in a way, are establishing a school for the service of character and country: emphatically not a "military academy," but (I transpose Benedict's words) "if a certain strictness results from the dictates of equity, for the amendment of vices or the preservation of charity, do not be dismayed...." We believe it to be the right and necessary way.

To live among very good people committed to something worthwhile, to watch them, to learn from them, to live according to an ideal that demands the suppression of ego in the service of larger purposes, most particularly to the fulfillment of our obligations to a community brought together for a common purpose, and with only the satisfaction of duty rendered according to our best talents, this is our best means of setting graduates on the way, preparing them to become the virtuous and disinterested citizens and leaders to which we are pledging ourselves.

I need say little more. In carrying out duties imposed, not by rules, but by their obligations to those who live among them and must depend upon them, our students will learn the humility and self-effacement that must be the concomitants of lives (if they are to be successful) that are spent doing battle in the world's fight. I want our students to stop thinking about themselves, about their entitlements and rights; I want them to consider their obligations and responsibilities. Those obligations will comprise a broad and differentiated family of regular tasks required to sustain a community like ours. Much of their work, their service, will be carried out very early in the mornings: young people *can* be habituated to this rather quickly, and for such purposes, it is indeed the best time of the day.

There is a huge family of services and chores to be attended to, day in, day out: the preparation of meals and maintenance of the refectories and their kitchens; the full maintenance of all the occupied areas of the demesne, including our buildings and the rude road networks that will link the villages; the rolling stock that we must maintain in all seasons; the students' own rooms and houses and public rooms must be kept up, as must the College's and villages' guest houses and apartments, and our own fire department and security detachments. Even certain parts of the large cattle ranch that adjoins the demesne (including looking after large animals, something most Americans cannot imagine, much less do) is a most useful inculcator of habits of regular attendance to needs that we, and we only, can answer. It is good for a young person to have to look after a big animal regularly. Such a list might be extended almost indefinitely.

I conclude with this observation: that it is in the performance of such work that our students will learn best both how to lead and how to follow. The word micromanaging, very much in the pejorative vogue nowadays, implies oversupervision. But there is another meaning, much more apposite: learning, by being charged with leading three or four or ten persons to do some tough manual or mechanical task, the most lasting lessons of leading others. I suppose, in another comparison, it is the kind of lesson generals can learn (and never forget) by serving in the lowliest ranks: lessons truly learned only by closest observation and unbuffered relations between young leaders and a very small number in their charge. You cannot learn those lessons by looking at large-scale maps, or by being student body president, and so on. I look sometimes at men like John McCain and Colin Powell, and I see instantly that here are two men that learned leading at the lowest and most elemental levels. And that is how our pupils will learn it, too; and run the College into the bargain.

Indeed, responsible leading must be learned and earned in emulation and practice, just as virtue, which is the core of responsible leading, is earned: by living in accordance with the instructions of conscience, and by working to emulate the exemplary legacies of those we study and the active examples of those from whom we learn.

Just as good character (according to Aristotle) is antecedent to effective rhetoric, virtue must precede responsible leadership. This must be an article of faith with us. This virtue is learned not by study but, as I have said, by the way the students will live. It is to be learned in a thousand small ways, most of them the kind of ways along which the young of our time are never directed: at 4:15 in the cold, blank darkness in one of the village refectory kitchens, where a shift of first- and second-year students, perhaps supervised by several fifth-years, are beginning to prepare (later they will serve) the day's breakfast; or on the third night of a fifty-two–mile overland Trek in the Medicine Bow Mountains, in which a student leader and an assigned assistant are trying to motivate, to keep moving, a ragged band of first-year students who have not eaten in several hours, and who are intimidated by both the difficult terrain and the prospect of another night in the cold.

Learning to Lead

This will be done in acts of confrontation on matters of honor; in the random internships, many assigned in venues and conditions of great stress, fatigue, and perhaps even danger; and in the daily acts of self-denial, forbearance, and tolerance that our students' communitarian living will exact from leaders and led alike: mending fences, mastering academic disciplines for which one has little aptitude—only by the volunteered tutorial efforts of friends (it is almost impossible that all our students will excel easily in all the required disciplines)—maintaining the physical conditions of the villages, performing the necessary and very often menial duties that the villages will demand. And virtually all will be accomplished with little acknowledgment save the thanks of friends and the satisfaction of completing worthwhile tasks. Individual allegiances to the teachings of revealed religion may link us to the Grace of knowing we are helping those who need our help; so may personal philosophies of what is good and worthwhile to do: to give and not to count the cost, to labor and not to seek for rest. These, the College maintains, are virtuous habits that belong in the interior lives and the active hands of our students. What to others might seem hardships will come to be accepted by us as habits; lives will be accordingly adjusted, expectations altered or diverted. Above all else, the *ethos* of service will be laid as the cornerstone of the edifice of effective and responsible leading.

The Sacramentum

When Americans think of oaths, they think of the Boy Scouts or of Hitler. They think of innocent pledges or avowals to do good, or of unequivocal commitments to do the bidding of the kind of leader who insists on oaths as guarantees of fidelity to him.

I can well imagine a student or two balking at "taking an oath" like ours. I am afraid that he will not be allowed to enroll. This is an embarrassment that may be avoided if the student is told of the ceremony and pledge at the time he is admitted to the College. Remember, Robert, we are an independent college, in receipt of no money whatever from local, state, or federal governments. Nor is it as though we will be asking new students to pledge their lives and their sacred honor—at least not their lives.

Our College should annually hold a chapel ceremony, at the opening of school, in which members of the entering cohort pledge themselves to the mission and purposes of the College. This is not to be a pledge to *someone*, or *even to the College*. The ceremony should be simple but moving. Members of the new cohort should recite their pledge before all other members of the College.

The College's hymn, "Once to Every Man and Nation," should be sung at the beginning of the ceremony. It should end with the anthem "O Beautiful for Spacious Skies" (a verse of which has an eerie appropriateness to our mission and *physical* setting), with the famous benediction from the Old Testament Book of Numbers ("the Lord Bless Thee and Keep Thee..."), and this prayer attributed to Ignatius Loyola:

For Generosity:
Teach Us, Dear Lord, to serve Thee as Thou Deservest.
To Give, and not to Count the Cost.
To Fight, and not to Heed the Wounds.
To Labor, and not to Seek for Rest.
To Serve Thee, and not Ask for Any Reward
Save that of Knowing that We Do Thy Will.

Religion at the College

"Consider the work of God: for who can make straight, which He hath made crooked?"

(Ecclesiastes, 7:13)

Of course the College is to be nonsectarian. But it is not to be nonreligious. On the contrary. "Unless the Lord buildeth the House, he labors in vain that builds it." I adduce the verse as fact and metaphor both. The final sanction of a firm religious faith—inspiration and prescription for how we live our lives and as foundation for our dedication to our country—lies at the heart of our mission.

As to basic, palpable things. I have mentioned a chapel for the College, and where I want it built. Its configuration should be such that it can accommodate the community fully and that it can be adapted efficiently according to the usages of various faiths or denominations. I expect the College to require regular attendance at divine services every Sabbath during terms of residence. In this regard, surely, all who matriculate will normally assent to the requirement as a condition of enrollment. I do not care what services they attend—within reason and our ability to provide the appropriate priest, minister, or rabbi—but what I do insist upon is that all attend services.

I insist on the primacy of religious faith in our community, including those, undoubtedly a majority, who have no strong denominated faith. For a majority of *them* understand in their hearts that there is a God, that He fathers forth in ways both multitudinous and transcendent, and that they are in some way to be touched, in their lives and perhaps after, by Him. It is a reflection common to adolescents; it ends usually in a shrug or a scowl of impatience or dismissal, but it is a reflection, an unbidden epiphany, to which they are all liable. I want the College to make them less impatient with it when it arrives.

I do not believe that those we hire to teach courses in religion should be chaplains, or that our chaplains should teach. And I am particularly interested in finding chaplains who, like our mentors and professors, will have answered their vocation rather late in their lives, having knocked and kicked around the world in other lines of work before. Here again: prefer the good man or the good woman to the smart or eloquent one. Of course you want both; but, above all, our chaplains must in their lives *show* what their faith has done for them, and what it can do for our pupils.

One of the colleges I know well insists in its charter that the president be an individual of an evangelical Christian religion. I do not care what religion our president is, by formal affiliation at least. And the word "evangelical" reminds me that the evangelism of personal example is for our purposes the most potent religious witness that we can set before our students. I do not want the chaplains trying to evangelize or convert students, save by their own living witness to their own faith. As I write this letter I am looking at a minister, faith not known, broadcasting from what appears to be a furniture showroom, wearing a wig, brandishing a jewelled pinkie ring, and decked out in two or three thousand dollars worth of aggressive suiting, in perfect forgetfulness of the lesson of the founder of the Christian religion.

To love brotherly without dissimulation, as John Winthrop preached, and to bring into common usage the avowed articles of religious creeds and professions. In other words, to be kind and forbearing, unself-regarding, in the way they live while at the College. This is the aim, the goal of the community in its work: to inculcate, by example, precept, and habit, a way of conduct so deeply planted and so bountifully nourished that it will mark out a way of living for every graduate of the College.

At the end of his life Winston Churchill's doctor wrote a long memoir. He made this observation about a twentieth-century Marcus Aurelius—George Marshall. "It was not what General Marshall *did*, but what he *was*, that lingers in the memory. His very goodness seemed to put ambition out of countenance." Now, Marshall was a soldier, hard as steel, unpretentious, quietly commanding, an embodiment of functional, organized duti- fulness. He would not, for example, even have *understood* how a man could call him a paragon of moral courage. His duty pre- scribed his behavior; to do one's duty was not a matter of courage, but of obligation. To live a life of service to our country, in accordance with such conviction, is both to render it the best service possible and to lay hold on the "very goodness" in whose nurture and education our College will find its highest calling.

Dear Robert,

I seem to remember a photograph of Teddy Roosevelt talking to another man, or rather listening to him, and in a peculiar and arresting way. He had his hand cupped around the back of the man's neck!—and was pulling him toward himself and at the same time, so it appeared, was squeezing information (or opinion or argument) out of him, so eager was he, TR, to hear and learn whatever it was the man was telling him.

It is a vivid image, absolutely characteristic. Somebody who hated Roosevelt might have said it was a metaphor for bullying, that TR was as ever importunate, intimidating. But I choose to see the image as representing something else: an ungovernable desire to learn something *at once*, an unquenchable avidity for fact, for knowledge, an unassuageable curiosity that remained as hearty in Roosevelt the president as it had been in TR the Harvard undergraduate. I imagine him as sustaining through life a boyish voracity: wanting to know and learn everything, always willing to listen, and to hear, before judging. No matter how passionate or partisan ("Honest partisanship is honest citizenship"), he wanted to know what his opponent, his antagonist, his rival, had to say; judgment could wait, even in him. You can be impetuous *after* you learn your facts.

I am thinking out loud, about ways by which we may inculcate in our students the lifelong habit of *listening creatively* and comfortably, and of *hearing* what they listen to in conversation. I once asked a friend at St. John's College to name something she was certain all graduates took with them when they left. She did not hesitate with her answer: "the habit of speaking up fearlessly in support of any belief or conviction, no matter who or what the audience was." Not a bad testimonial—how many colleges can argue the same result. Two, three, five? Only places where discourse is raw delight, and where it goes on ceaselessly among people who like each other and who don't let opinions and convictions erupt friendships. You remember what Mill said: there can be no philosophy where fear of consequences is greater than love of truth.

Speaking up fearlessly and the Hell with tact. There is no need for tact in the context I imagine for the College. No one would know what it was, or what to do with it. Equally no one should leave our College without the cultivated habit of avid listening, without prejudgment or rage or irritability, to opinions as different from his own as can be. The great master of the subject is Montaigne: "I embark upon discussion and argument with great ease and liberty. Since opinions do not find in me a ready soil to thrust and spread their roots into, no premise shocks me, no belief hurts me, *no matter how opposite to my own they may be... when I am contradicted it arouses my attention, not my wrath.*"

Somehow we have to build into the culture and curriculum of the College some means of habituating—that is the only word for it I can think of—habituating our pupils to pungent, aggressive conversation whose main feature may be disagreement without disagreeableness.

To bring them together at the College, when they are young and embarking upon a common enterprise, and, moreover, to be led and taught by teachers whose joy in teaching them is palpable, and who themselves do not resent disagreement, this is the great prerequisite. Among the horrendous depredations of what we call "political correctness," the worst is watching our mouth for fear of giving offense, i.e., I will no longer impute good will to you if something you say *seems* (whatever it is) somehow to be connected invidiously with my sex or my country or my race or my faith, if I have any. Even in the act of saying what I have just said I have foreclosed the amiable attention of half the people that nowadays make their living in the academy, because they sense in it some coded signal that I, Adams, am "a conservative."

I seem to come back, always, to the question of teachers, or professors. For in our College their lives will be lived among our students, and the chief means of communicating this lesson—this lesson in listening, learning, arguing without rancor or residue of resentment—must be their example. They must be steadfast in conviction, passionate in enunciation of belief, debonair in the way they wear their knowledge and in the way they end their conversations.

There was a man whose name I do not recall, but who I somehow think may have been a Quaker. He believed that, if you did not like someone, or if you sensed he did not like you, you should make yourself go up to him and shake his hand, engage him in some trifling way, build upon that, deliberately and watchfully making yourself a friend. I have gone on too long, but I sense in this act a kind of metaphor for how we should make ourselves learn to converse, when we find ourselves (as our pupils surely will) pitted against opinions so different from our own that they cannot but impute sorry motives to their holder.

In the way you and the other founding trustees set about organizing the College, this is counsel which I hope you will take strenuously to heart. It is surely in mine.

Look forward to hearing from you. The army is on the move again.

As ever,
John Adams

*D*EAR MR. ADAMS,

Thank you for "How Should They Live?" Your answer is that they should live strenuously, hard, and in the "bracing air of the Great Plains." My wife agrees, make them all be in charge of a horse or some other large animal—our daughter (the girl that wants to go to Brown) has a young Arabian, and we believe it has been good for her.

Do the students ever receive strokes? she asks. Remember that word, from Nixon days, stroking? Or is their only fuel knowing that they have done right? I don't mean to imply grade inflation—just something that lets them know they're making good and visible progress.

You are the donor, so I withhold comment on the separate housing for men and women. I see what you are trying to do, and of course the board will instruct the first administration to do it that way. But in 2000, or whenever the first classes actually get to the site, will such rules be enforceable? I do not applaud or condone the current Washington shenanigans, but, in the old line, what are we to tell the children? How are we to expect that they remain chaste?

I have retained the architects that you have specified, and they will visit you, in Douglas, next Friday.

Robert Parkman

Dear Robert,

Watching late in pain. This morning I sat on the veranda in the bright, flat March sunlight, the prospect away to the east russet and undusty, the air of a clarity that singed the skin. I read St. Paul to the Romans. My housekeeper appeared, to warn me about skin cancer! Now it is 2 AM, eighteen hours later; black and still, and the new protocol has me synaesthetic—that is, *seeing* colors of pain, *hearing* its buffets batter by. I see him all the same as an enemy, this cancer pain, a patient, canny enemy— Boers or North Vietnamese—always in silent preparation for his next assault, bombardment, reconnaissance. Always there.

I wonder whether Marcus Aurelius or George Marshall would acknowledge pain—in a letter to, say, Fronto or Omar Bradley? (But such men had colleagues, not friends, and "feelings are something I reserve for Mrs. Marshall.") I seem to see in the bottlegreen haze of screensaver-glow some sort of liquid peering eye, scrutinizing me, sizing me up: Pain, said Emily Dickinson, has an element of blank, and cannot recollect when it began, or (even) if there was a time when it was not. The cancer, dear Robert, has eaten its way well into bone (which is why I had the one-time radiation treatment done last week, in Cheyenne). Doctor, as Mrs. Hamill refers to him, will be here tomorrow; my mother used the same locution—"Doctor" is coming, like spring is coming or rain is coming—and thus is the probably (no, certainly) dying man reconnected to the little boy, who had his schools, his war, the love of his life and his bereavement, his whole life before him. But you were living before that... and now, you are living after. This cancer is rambunctiously invasive, a force of guerrillas in a swamp, like an army of the Great War that has broken through our rusty line, has gotten into our reserve trenches, is now running amok looking for loot, souvenirs, prisoners: unimpeded, berserk. My new analgesic protocol, once thought indifferent in the counterattack, is holding up reasonably well—most of the time, but not just now.... But I am not being the man I want you to think I am.

Attached is "What Should They Learn?" Let me see if I can gather myself to put down something that's important to our College, at least as I see it.

Yours,
John Adams

CHAPTER 5

What Should They Learn?

THE RICH HATRED THAT SUBSISTED between Sparta and Athens assured that their war would be a long one, and that it would last until one side felt itself defeated utterly. At the end of the first year of the war, in 430 B.C., Pericles, first citizen of Athens, spoke at a funeral honoring those killed in the fighting, using the occasion less to remember those who had died than to celebrate the character of the city for which they had fought. He asked those in his audience to "fix [their] eyes every day on the greatness of Athens as she really is, and fall in love with her. When you realize her greatness, then reflect that what made her great was men with a spirit of adventure, men who knew their duty, men who were ashamed to fall below a certain standard." And he reminded them that their "love of the beautiful does not lead to extravagance," any more than "their love of things of the mind makes them soft." As for money, "we regard it as something to be properly used, rather than as something to be boasted about." Further, as Athenians they are "capable at the same time of taking risks and of estimating them beforehand." Everyone is "able to show himself, in all the manifold aspects of life, both the rightful lord and master of his own person, and to do this with exceptional grace and versatility." And in Athens, finally:

Each individual is interested not only in his own affairs but in the affairs of the state as well; even those who are mostly occupied with their own business are extremely well informed on general politics—this is a peculiarity of ours: we do not say that a man who takes no interest in politics is a man who minds his own business, we say that he is a man who has no business at all.

In the mission for our College we speak of "preparation" of certain kinds of citizens, instead of *education* or *training*. But I mean for the word to comprise both, indeed to fuse their purposes, just as our work will fuse the purposes of civic education with that form of education we call liberal. My premise is that the best and most useful citizens are ideally also those best educated—as intellectuals, as students of history and letters, as scientists, mathematicians, doctors, writers, executives. But they will also have been *trained*, schooled to their obligations as American citizens, and as citizens at the numberless levels of *communitas* that distinguish our country.

It is a gigantic idealism, of course. So far as the great affairs of the nation are concerned, the tendency of American citizens of our age is toward an enthralled, titillated fascination, shame, or uninterest; and its corollary is the private indulgence of lives that separate them from any communitarian obligation. Such obligations (we no longer call them that) are remote, if acknowledged at all. Great national issues seem hopelessly unresponsive to the frail efforts of ordinary citizens—those efforts for which we have any energy after the draining spasms of frantic work we employ to advance ourselves in our own professions. The Greek citizen whom Pericles extols—his needs attended to, his country smaller than Rhode Island, his citizen cohort less than 25,000—lived in a world starkly different from ours.

Yet the College, its small means and small population acknowledged, must consecrate itself toward a revival of precisely those fused virtues that Pericles cherished in his city. Training ourselves to do those things our citizenship obliges, whether we want to do them or not, and learning to become self-educating for the rest of our lives—such missions should not be at strife. The College must demand excellence in many things. It must inculcate habits of tenacity and determination—the unseen prerequisites to "exceptional grace and versatility." Devotion to community, demonstrated and lived in an habitual willingness to put community ahead of self, is an obvious prerequisite to "preparation for virtuous and disinterested service." And yet all that we ask of our students should be seen as interfused, our requirements seamlessly complementary. We see no antipathy between education and training; we should see none, either, between that kind of education called civic and that form of education appropriately called liberal.

Much earlier I set down a list of qualities of character and mind that I wanted state committees on admission to look for in candidates. These are all virtues the College community in its manifold activities may cultivate and strengthen—and perhaps even instill. They are readily linked to the virtues Pericles imputes to his idealized Athenians:

1. Unself-conscious moral courage.
2. Self-forgetfulness and self-mastery.
3. Indifference to material success and to "things."
4. Fierce patriotism.
5. Willingness to assume responsibility without calculation of risk or reward.
6. Intellectual self-reliance; independence of judgment.
7. Retention of a lifelong sense of wonder.
8. Magnanimity, liberality, generosity.
9. Physical hardihood and resistance to fatigue.

Pericles exhorts his citizens to fix their attention on the greatness of their city. "Fall in love with her." No doubt, as disinterested citizens, they and we may diagnose flaws and ills, but we must labor with a will to correct them, and not allow "the age we live in" to make us cynical.

Pericles asks us to think upon what, and who, made their country great. Our citizens, like the Athenians, must know our common history, its origins, evolution, and the truly great who have always served and led those who went before. We have remarked that the core of a proper education for an earlier generation of Americans was the idea of emulation. Do not merely admire. Resolve to use in your own life that which you praise in another's. The citizens of Pericles' city are to learn the nature of the standards of conduct and enterprise beneath which they should be ashamed to fall.

It is in the nature of our cultivated humanity to learn and to do many things well, and to move from one to another without fuss, with a becoming ease, and with a delight in the accomplishments that our education, our talent, and our industry will make possible: "exceptional grace and versatility," or what the Italians call *sprezzatura*, usefully rendered as "effortless superiority." And when citizens fail to shoulder their duties to their country, their education is to be identified as a primary cause of that failure. It has allowed them to think that a successful management of their own pursuits alone is a sufficient occupation for a fulfilled and honorable life.

The College's mission is an unusual one. We have already considered the things that distinguish it from the stated missions of other colleges. On the other hand, most of the academic components of the education I propose, though unusual in the proportions I am assigning them, are neither unusual nor unfamiliar. They are subsumed in liberal education, a way of education that embodies a family of aims known to all. They will serve the needs of our mission, and of our students, well. They will make them alive to people and things that are noble and exquisite, and to those that are ignoble, coarse, or unworthy; to (in the famous formulation, never bettered) "the best that has been said and thought in the world," but also to the darkest and most hateful designs and works of man; to what is excellent, to the means by which excellence is pursued and achieved, and to the satisfactions that laboring and living to such ends may bestow.

The curriculum proposed will serve the requirements to which our civic mission summons us. Like Aristotle's and Pericles' ideal citizenry, and like Thomas Jefferson's vision of what American citizens in their best selves should be, our graduates must be citizens educated and determined to attain and to realize their fullest humanity as citizens, not as self-absorbed calculators of their own advantage, self-indulgent recluses, slaves to their professions, to advancement, to money.

But let me state simply what I believe should be the academic staples of our curriculum. Let me propose their proportions in that curriculum. A few will demand a brief apologia or explanation; others a listing of subsidiary courses. The College's mission should be borne in mind.

Major Topics or Fields of Study

History	30%
Foreign Languages	20%
Mathematics	10%
Science	10%
Philosophy, Theology, Deontology	10%
Composition/Rhetoric	10%
Imaginative Literature	5%
Music and Fine Arts	5%

These percentages should suggest numbers of courses taken, individual studies, "contact hours" with mentors and professors for each topic. Since each full year of on-demesne tuition provides two full terms and two interims, I see twelve "courses" being offered in that year: five per term, and one for each interim—the latter typically an immersion in one of the two required foreign languages, and the kind of immersion in which students enrolled would "live" in the language as well as study it. But though the percentages should suggest courses taken, they are not to be understood as precise representations of their general importance, or of the total time our students may devote to them. Of course the topics "bleed" into one another throughout. For example: much of the foreign language curriculum as I envision it would be taught through the literatures, histories, and contemporary political cultures of the countries to which the languages studied are native. Or consider that among the languages to be offered are Greek and Latin. The College's huge requirement in history (the equivalent by itself of what most schools would call a double major) should among other topics comprise courses in the histories of classical Greece, the Roman Republic, and the Roman Empire— all three. To understand that history there is no surer aid than a knowledge of one or both classical languages, Latin especially. As well expect the fullest value from reading Tolstoy or Turgenev in English, as from reading Tacitus or Sallust in any language other than that in which he thought, lived, and wrote. The program in composition and rhetoric is most aptly served by requiring students to study models of functional, precise, graceful prose. I think at once of the *Gallic Wars* or of the *Agricola*. The first is set down in language as functional and spare as the working parts of a Roman catapult; the second, in Latin, as noble, as simple in its stateliness, as the constitution of the Republic itself. And who will doubt that history, as I envisage its academic presentation at our College, is, truly, literature. I think of history in the grand narrative tradition that engages and enthralls even as it provokes and educates: good, thick, nourishing soups, not the kind of tepid gruel now being served to, and regularly shunned by, undergraduate students.

Hard-earned knowledge in one academic field, the consequence of prolonged immersion in that field and its many presentations, is a potent agent for the development of what we defined, much earlier, as disinterestedness. It is linked reliably to the growth of a comfortable self-reliance and independence in reaching our own judgments, and in maintaining and asserting them. We learn to trust our own counsel. The poet Hopkins noted that "the effect of studying a classic is to make me admire, and do otherwise." The avid student and master of history, Winston Churchill, did not hesitate to stand up in the House of Commons after Chamberlain's triumphal return from Munich, and, before five hundred members, to assert: "I say we have sustained a tragic and unmitigated defeat." The disinterested person and citizen is far less likely to be cowed by tactical considerations or seduced by his political fears than his uneducated colleague. So far as our purpose holds to prepare citizens and leaders in government, I know no better preparation for lives of self-reliant intellection than an immersion, beginning as early in life as possible, in history.

I want our graduates to cultivate and retain through their lives a sense of wonder. The statement seems harmless, a bromide. But how many adults, Robert, can you name, adults in the world of affairs, who have retained the delighted freshness of response to things new to them, the unclouded delight in the singular things each day flings before them: strange architectures, frissons of wit, symphonies, inventions, strategies, pictures, the wisdom of children? Strangely, you may think, I find such receptivities far more common among my dear friends (and former colleagues) who are engineers at Carswell, who work in an environment in which the bounds of the possible are extended daily, and in which their delight inheres in being both reconnoiterers and exploiters of what lies beyond them. Do not take refuge beyond the tedious "two cultures" dichotomy, asserting that since men cannot change, then we are relieved of any obligation to think, hard, endlessly, about how we may improve the way they live together. No, the truth is that we are jaded and exhausted by our work; we are dandled by the levellers who feed us information and entertain us; we are patronized by men of commerce who pander to our desperate need to conform—to opinion we fear to offend, and to taste we fear to ignore. When was the last time your heart leaped up, at anything?

There is a homely story about Vladimir Horowitz, which I cannot confirm: that he insisted on giving concerts only on Sunday afternoons (there were other specifications too), because he knew that men dragged to evening concerts by their wives (this was many a year ago, of course) were (1) exhausted and (2) even more refractory than usual—in their resistance to having to listen to... one need not continue.

The fact is that no one can be liberally educated. The phrase we must use always—if it truly reflects our conviction—is *liberally self-educating*. Unless our graduates have left the demesne more avid for education of the kind I propound than when they arrived, five years earlier, we have failed them, and they have failed themselves.

As organized, the calendar I propose to the board and the first leaders of the College offers between forty and forty-five blocs of time for the study of courses assigned within the eight subjects, or topics, proposed. There are virtually no electives (an obvious exception is in foreign languages); and the on-the-ground founders, in a year or two, will have to decide how best to distribute the courses among these "blocs." Certain subjects will have to be prerequisite to others; certain subjects will make comfortable or synergistic coevals of others. I do not wish to prescribe too closely, but I cannot resist making a suggestion or two:

The first is that the College must always keep *our* mission in view when it decides how to assign and arrange the academic curriculum's various topics and courses. The second is that you must remember that you will not be enrolling well-educated boys and girls. You will be able to assume little about their education to this point, and that is why, earlier, I suggested that the College might make the best possible use of the period between the student's admission and his matriculation—those ten months in which, we may say, the student is braced to his prospects and challenges. The third is that their academic obligations will be significant, but so will their other commitments—particularly in the way they are going to be living and in their training out-of-doors, abroad, and in the houses and villages. One of the things that makes me confident that the program will function well is that those who will superintend its work, including the great majority of our teachers, will themselves have obligations to missions other than academic ones—obligations they understand to be complementary to the academic, not *competitive* with them.

To be more specific: I do not think courses in the philosophy, theology, deontology curriculum should be offered early in the

student's five-year *cursus*. The grand catechistic questions—
"What is Truth?" "What is Virtue?" "What is the Nature of
Man," and so forth—are best delayed a year or two, until students are comfortable in their College environment and, more
important, have shown the capacity to analyze, to think clearly,
to write and speak with some confidence and precision. I well
remember my first tutorials at Cambridge: the gnomic, impenetrable intelligence of my tutor and my rank inability to come
to terms with it, to engage "it." (Even now I remember my
interlocutor as an "it" rather than a "he," so remote from all I
had learned to that point were the premises of his queries, one
of which was that I knew what I was talking about. I knew
nothing.) Those huge Aspen questions, those gamy staples of
the Leisure of the Theory Class, are the most urgent and timeless of all—therefore, let them wait for eighteen months.

The opening orientation month—I shall address this a bit
later—is a time both ideal and necessary for the work of assuring
a full computer literacy among all new members of Cohort I.
That seems obvious enough. For the same reasons it seems
inescapable that the composition portion of our Subject Area
#1 be introduced early—say, for the first two terms of a *cursus*.
The majority of the cohort cannot write a simple English sentence, much less utter one, and that will have to be fixed early. I
also think you must have your math up front. And work on the
first of the two required foreign languages will have to begin early.

Last: I would teach painting in the first term, not only
because it is a discipline that relies on different talents and
expectations, but also because it can provide certain early satisfactions of the kind young students crave and need.

The founding board may take issue with my curriculum,
arguing for electives, wondering why there is no anthropology

or economics, or no sequence of courses in computers, chemistry, or business. The answer is that I have tried to make a fixed curriculum that best serves the mission, as I have conceived it. There is a corollary. The mind does not recognize academic boundaries. Descartes was a delighted student of mathematics (on his own) and Oppenheimer an amateur poet. "Courses" in one subject do not imply a lifelong debility in a subject not taken. In the microprocessor business there is a gigantic range of eccentric and variegated academic backgrounds among the industry's wisest and most productive leaders and scientists. And I remember a far grimmer but perhaps not less apposite item of advice, given me in Hawaii two months before we landed on Iwo Jima: at night, in uncertain light, look slightly to the left or right, look slightly away, from the object you are trying to make out. You see it best that way.

I attach, Robert, notations I have made for several of the topics that I want the College to offer.

History: The Idea of Emulation

Please remember, as you read through these pages, that I am talking about the study of history as it is to be carried on at our College, given *our* mission and my understanding of our purposes. Incontestably, history is our most important academic subject. In the way we define and present the discipline to our students, we will determine its success or its failure.

And "success," never fully measurable in such matters, means that inculcation of a lifelong love of history, particularly the history of our country, in every student who enrolls in the College and becomes its graduate. Perhaps a *permanent passion* for history more accurately describes what I am after. I want our men and women to act with instinctive and educated reference to what their study of history has taught and is teaching them; bringing to bear on the decisions of their lives and work, their serving and leading, diagnostic resources not so different from those—for his profession—of a canny old country GP, a general practitioner. I do not imply an ability or a trained habit or trying to make simple comparisons or simple-minded inferences from political history; I do mean the self-educating habit of taking decisions with reference to what our minds and memories instruct us has worked, or failed, in the past. I am thinking in terms of what you would call, generally, biographical. For when we learn about justice, about courage, about suffering, about patriotism, we learn best when we learn such as they exalt or crush *individual* lives, men and women we have come to know. Robert: is there a man in history that you love, whose life somehow seems to speak directly to your own consciousness, whose life, with its sorrows and exaltations, somehow means something to the way you live your own? A life you can somehow "realize"?

Everything that "history" is becoming seems to me to be what it should not be at our College. As an academic discipline professed by college teachers, its purposes strike me as careerist, antiquarian, and out-of-joint with the real needs of undergraduate students who are going to be bankers, doctors, executives, politicians, lawyers—but almost invariably *not* history professors. Of course most newly minted professors have never thought through the question of what they are teaching history *for*, or to *whom* they will be teaching it. Too many are but learned drones and graceless writers who do not understand human character, because they have themselves been remote from the real living-and-breathing commodity. Their aims strike me as dissective rather than synthetic: aims conditioned, I imagine, in the graduate schools and by the stated missions of the learned periodicals for which they feel themselves bound to produce articles. I also find the current neurosis—the notion that those in our American history who once led our forbearers must be judged according to the standards of our time only, and not their own—appalling: no doubt a consequence of the current diffidence about saying anything good about any deceased white American, Abraham Lincoln excepted, without apology. Finally, I see almost no history being written as it should be: as historical narrative of propulsive momentum, narrative that is both inclusive and accurate but also written with some solicitude for the needs of the intelligent lay reader (who, if anyone, is the person for whom such work should be written). That, you will say, is an issue much larger than any we can address. That is true. But in your selection of the books that our students should be asked to read and to understand, you and our colleagues on our first history faculty can do much to rectify the unhappy practice of our own time.

Let me register here, also, my inability to understand the low, low caste to which military history has always been relegated in our American historiography, and perhaps never lower than now. If there were ever a time in which our students should be made to understand why men fight, and how they organize themselves for fighting, and what truths and lies they feed themselves and their enemies when they fight, that time is now. Yet no one studies war. And we are at one of history's hinges, too, in which the character of war appears to be changing, partly for reasons that are technical, partly for reasons that have to do with the growing inability of nation-states to address the needs of the people living within their own borders. And yet military historians, with an exception or two, are ignored in the academy, as are their works past and current.

I do not see that the world we inhabit is fundamentally different from the world described by the greatest historian who ever wrote, the world of jostling, angry sovereignties that was the Greece of the fifth century. I frankly expect us to go to war, often, and soon, and I expect that within fifteen years we will be at war with China—we with our allies against China with its. The United Nations is no more effectual in removing the irritants that start the wars than was the Delian League. So short is our memory, however, and so averse to learning from history is our temperament, that we cannot imagine such horrors happening again; and in a way that implicates us directly, and that will terribly vindicate the prophecies of historians and philosophers. It is a baleful prediction, but an accurate one, I am sure.

The histories of Greece and Rome are profoundly instructive. This is a statement like the following: the ocean is full of fish. In so many ways, in their aspirations and expectations, in their self-denials and self-indulgences, in their ascendancy to an international imperium and their collapse from causes that seem to us now "inevitable"; above all in the extraordinary *dramatis personae* of leaders history has plucked from the dreck, they offer us vivid, frightening images of ourselves, and of what our own civilization is, pell-mell, becoming. Soon after the Romans under Sulla had defeated Mithradates (84 B.C.), Sulla asked, "Now that the universe offers us no more enemies, what may be the fate of the Republic?" The Romans learned their fate within three generations; are we capable of using what we have learned, from understanding the histories of Rome, of Greece, of other countries in situations not unlike our own, led by men no different from ours, capable of using to advantage the lessons that are there for the picking?

A chestnut of amateur debate is the question of American Talent and Leadership, 1770–1810. It is a heightened, more profound version of the admiral's query in *The Bridges at Toko-Ri*: How did we find such men? Dr. Commager frames the question: How did the frontier colony of Virginia produce, in one generation, George Washington, George Mason, Patrick Henry, James Madison, Thomas Jefferson, and George Wythe? At a time when their coadjutors included Benjamin Franklin, John Adams, and Alexander Hamilton? The historian reminds us that the clichés are insufficient explanation: great challenges draw forth great talents; (or) the best talents have nowhere else to go, to serve, in such days. But does he find part of the answer in the Founders' education? They were soaked in the history of Rome and of Greece, and they studied Greek and Latin. They knew their Bible; they were children of the political philosophers of the Enlightenment. They had for the most part no degrees, as they had, for the most part, no university education. Yet they thought more clearly, considered more self-reliantly, wrote more accurately and eloquently, than we. Central to their education and to that of their children was the idea of emulation: of—quite literally—making the best features of an historical person's life their own. The premise was that we can learn lessons, moreover learn them in ways that will permanently influence our own conduct, from the lives of those who have gone before: particularly in the ways they faced crises in their own and in their countries' lives, most particularly in their self-mastery. The premise seems to be timeless, the relevance to our own day brutally direct.

Robert, remember the words of Plutarch:

> …[V]irtue by the bare statement of its actions, can so affect men's minds as to create at once both admiration of the thing done and the desire to imitate the doers of them. The goods of fortune we would possess and would enjoy;

those of virtue we long to practice and exercise... moral good is a practical stimulus: it is no sooner seen, than it inspires an impulse to practice and influence the mind and character.

Thirty percent of our pupils' academic time is to be given to the study of history. A horseback calculation yields fourteen or fifteen courses—including the history of the country to which they will be assigned for their term abroad for language study—or course equivalents. I have further suggested the importance to our mission of the idea of emulation—the study of men and women in history whose lives are, personally and individually, significant to us: persons whose lives as we know them will offer us lessons that, by the alchemy of intellectual disposition, interest, the lapse of time, we somehow may come to incorporate in our own characters. We do become parts of all that we have met, and we may be inspired, chastened, improved, *changed* by prior lives whose achievements (and the cost of those achievements) have left us legacies through our understanding of them. Again: I do not imply hero worship—far from it. Nor do I mean a naive acceptance, uncritical and blindly devotional, of what uncontested panegyric tells us of the great. I simply trust—hope—that the culture of history at our College will exclude the terrible corrosiveness, the snotty, arid, nasty temper of so much contemporary scholarship and history writing. Scholars today—so far from seeking to understand how men have lived and worked, their motives and their affections, their ambitions and the premises on which they made their choices— set out to attack, to tear apart, to demolish and trample upon reputations, always applying the standards and expectations—as they understand them—of our age to their subjects'.

Emulation. I have written also about military history and its importance in our curriculum, and its absence from those of most universities. Americans cannot imagine that they will go to war again (something a resurrected Tocqueville would surely note about us), and so they do not study the phenomenon, and discourage their children from enrolling in the armed forces, or of studying war themselves. Our College will not perpetuate such naive foolishness.

The curriculum should include courses in the history of classical Greece, with concentration on the political practices and culture of Athenian democracy and its rivals, and upon the long war fought against Sparta. As much of the subject that can be studied through contemporary sources and writers should be engaged in that way; and of course Thucydides must be read whole: the purest, most honorable, judicious, and reliable historian who ever wrote. And there should be courses in the history of Rome, from the beginnings to the end of the Republic; and from the beginnings of the Augustan principate to the fall of the empire in the West. Again: the Roman historians themselves should be read, in Latin where possible, by all students—Livy, Sallust, and Tacitus, in particular. It is unthinkable that an educated American citizen not consider carefully the character of the Roman Republic, the causes, meaning, and results of its dissolution. Everything I see in our own national life suggests to me a common course, a common descent into the very qualities of our corporate national life that doomed the great character and legacy of the Republic: not least, as we have noted, our inability to determine how to behave—"What Is Our Mission?"—in a world in which we are the only superpower, but in which our own citizenry cannot be bothered to vote in elections to the American presidency. You call this apocalyptic musing; I call it objective assessment.

There should be a year-long course in world history; and our students should be encouraged to concentrate, in that year, on the history of the country to which they will be sent for the term abroad. I think we are wise to follow the gamin's counsel of Lytton Strachey: to lower a single bucket very deep into a large lake, examining those contents with great care, rather than staring into the depths all around, as we try to "cover" the whole lake. We should work to know, as well as human agency permits, one culture other than our own.

Consider, for obvious reasons, requiring courses in the history of Europe and in the history of Britain.

The familiar two-term sequence in the history of our own nation cannot be avoided. I do not, of course, *want* to avoid it; but I am thinking that we cannot trust to the prior education of our students to have taught them to learn and begin to understand the history and heritage of their own land. Particular courses, typically of a term's duration, should fasten upon the great, if extended, events in our common history: the Revolution (which might end with the installation of the Washington administration, in 1789, and should surely include a careful study of the making of the Constitution); the Civil War (including Reconstruction); the Great Depression and World War II; Vietnam and Civil Rights—the last a tandem that seems to me sensible, when you consider it. One-half of the history requirement should be in American history.

Our aim is to create for students a lifelong avocation in history. The ideal is that at forty our graduates will remain as avid for historical knowledge and wisdom as when they leave our demesne. One means is to fire students' imaginations with works of history that are compelling narratives. To read Henry

Adams, to know Bancroft, Parkman, Beard, Parrington, D.S. Freeman, Dumas Malone, and the contemporary works of historians like Remini, Joseph Ellis, and Gordon Wood, is not only to allow ourselves to be engaged, as active and critical students and readers, it is also to grant ourselves entry to a world so capacious, so rightly evoked, so full of instruction, that we can imagine no more useful guide to the times we inhabit.

[I once asked Adams whether he was conscious of emulating anyone in history. Men nowadays smile, as he said, at the very preposterousness of the notion—their every tendency being to discover what hideous or evil things they had done, or how they had been lackeys of the Ruling Capitalism, and such. But Plutarch wrote with the intention that his heroes be emulated. The generations before that of the Founding Fathers subscribed utterly to the notion—finding in the noble Romans of the late Republic those most apt for the purpose. Adams did not smile. He took my question with perfect seriousness.

He said something like this: You learn a man's life, and you are not conscious of having been influenced by that life until you have known it well, and for some time, its dark corners and disasters as well as its triumphs, and particularly those of its tragedies that historians, in their patronizing and unfeeling way, like to call "personal," as though such things were nothing but speedbumps on the Great One's Turnpike to Eminence. Adams referred me to a comment of James Michener's, to the effect that an heroic life must pit the hero against himself as well as the other challenges he must master. Like a ship, such a man moves best when he is "slightly athwart the wind. Like ships, men do poorly when the wind is directly behind, pushing them... so that no care is required in steering...."

With two exceptions, he said, he was not conscious of emulating an individual life. The exceptions, one of them familiar to us already, included Marcus Aurelius and Sir Thomas More. Adams knew and read all there was to know and to read about (and by) these men. It is not hard to see what commended them to him. Their nobility, the nobility of giving honest service, for a very long time, to a most difficult but worthy mission, without whining, without the satisfactions on which most men depend, allegiant to ideals and ready to die for them. Their patriotism. You might know such men so well, he said, that you could absorb and fuse something of the essence of their character into your own.

Singular acts of bravery or magnanimity might find permanent lodgment in the memory, and these could inspire, move, prompt echoing actions. In an e-mail Adams talked of Anwar Sadat and his willingness to embrace the Ancient Enemy for peace's sake. He was undone, not a year before he died, by the story of King Hussein of Jordan, who had fallen on his knees before the families of seven Israeli daughters, all killed by a deranged Jordanian soldier—Hussein begging the forgiveness of these families in the name of his own people. He cherished the story, so he said, of Kemal Attaturk, who, asked by the bereaved English relatives of men killed fighting against his army (Attaturk's) at Gallipoli, if they could build a memorial to their dead on Turkish soil, replied: Only if I am allowed to write the epitaph—the epitaph to and for your sons. And in the epitaph he said that those lads, having died on Turkish ground, had become his sons as well.

Such sublime acts of courage and magnanimity retain a capacity, always fresh if we allow it to be, to inspire us, and to make us perhaps better. At the College, Adams insisted, it was our business to sustain such legacies and never, never, to explain them away. "Murder to dissect," he called the process. We may all of us emulate men and women from history—as we do persons known to us in our own lives. We are emulating the best of a wholeness, not usually a particular episode. More than anything else we are emulating the quality—call it, simply, character—that enables some very few to surmount hardship, loss, privation, danger, and for a long time, simply to serve an ideal. Have we lost that, he wondered, in America? Have we?

He kept this poem on his desk:

"The Truly Great," by Stephen Spender

I think continually of those who were truly great.
Who, from the womb, remembered the soul's history
Through corridors of light where the hours are suns,
Endless and singing. Whose lovely ambition
Was that their lips, still touched with fire,
Should tell of the spirit clothed from head to foot in song.
And who hoarded from the spring branches
The desires falling across their bodies like blossoms.

What is precious is never to forget
The delight of the blood drawn from ancient springs
Breaking through rocks in worlds before our earth;
Never to deny its pleasure in the simple morning light,
Nor its grave evening demand for love;
Never to allow gradually the traffic to smother
With noise and fog the flowering of the spirit.

Near the snow, near the sun, in the highest fields
See how these names are feted by the waving grass,
And by the streamers of white cloud,
And whispers of wind in the listening sky;
The names of those who in their lives fought for life,
Who wore at their hearts the fire's center.
Born of the sun, they travelled a short while towards the sun
And left the vivid air signed with their honor.

—R.P.]

[In a discussion I had with him two weeks before he died, Adams said he hoped the College would offer a course on the Plains Indians, the tragic saga of their lives and culture, from the coming of white men down to the present. He also gave me a memorandum he'd written that morning about another course he hoped we'd teach. I reprint it here, verbatim:

Germany, 1914–1945
Schumann's *Traumerei* is played hourly over the unmarked graves of 600,000 Russians in St. Petersburg's largest cemetery. The composer's countrymen killed them.

I envision this course as a study of the relationship between German "culture," broadly conceived; German militarism; and the wars Germany loosed on the world in August 1914 and September 1939. The course should, of course, examine the roots of genocidal anti-Semitism, the character of the German resistance to Hitler, and the reality of the death camps. Special topics might include the nature of Hitlerian tyranny; the Berlin demimonde, 1925–1940; the major military campaigns; and Church versus Regime, 1934–1945.

—R.P.]

Foreign Languages

When he was very young, T.E. Lawrence (the famous Lawrence of Arabia) lived with his family in Brittany. He learned French with easy and almost immediate fluency, as children do in such circumstances, and, as Jeremy Wilson puts it:

As a result he never felt the apprehension about living in foreign countries that was so common among the British. Lawrence later wrote that [the British] reinforced their national character "by memories of the life they have left. In reaction against their foreign surroundings they take refuge in the England that was theirs."... Lawrence was to become one of those Englishmen who, in his own words, "feel deeply the influence of the native people, and try to adjust themselves to its atmosphere and spirit... they imitate the native as far as possible, and so avoid friction in their daily life...."

Americans, for reasons too tedious to rehearse, are little different from those British whose "national character" tends to be reinforced by work and travel abroad and by the study of foreign cultures, countries, and languages. How many times in my life have I seen our countrymen abroad *shouting* out words in our tongue, repeating them louder and louder before "foreigners," in the ridiculous hope that they will thus make themselves understood? How many times have I winced when our employees, abroad or at home with foreign visitors, have had to make shamefaced apologies for the ignorance of any language but their own, only to be reassured by their guests—crisply in serviceable English—that this will not pose a problem.

But there are more important considerations that impel the College's insistence that its students master foreign languages— specifically, two of them.

The first is obvious. Those in our first cohort will have been born around 1985 or 1986. They will live to a time within two or three decades of the twenty-second century. It is likely they will live, serve, or work abroad—often for long periods—and it is no good saying that, by then, everyone will be speaking English, if they aren't already. Clearly our countrymen will discharge their duties, not only to their companies, but also to our country, and to themselves with far greater efficiency and credibility if they know the language of their hosts, or if they are eager and active learners of their hosts' language, just as they should be avid students of their hosts' country itself. While our national arrogance manifests itself less curtly than the Englishman's, its normal presentation, the shrugging, ingratiatory confession of ignorance, is doubly shaming and often crippling.

And this compels my second argument: our students must study languages for what they may teach us about ourselves—ourselves as ordinary men and women and Americans, but also as members of the larger human community, as it has lived through history and will live when our generation is gone. Goethe is said to have remarked, "Who knows not another language knows not his own"; Macaulay, remembering Charles V, reminded us that to learn *any* new language and learn it well was to acquire a new soul. "New Associations take place among the student's ideas. He doubts where he formerly dogmatized. He tolerates where he formerly execrated. He ceases to confound what is universal and eternal in human passions and opinions with what is local and temporary. This is one of the most useful effects which results from studying the literature of other countries."

The languages I think should be offered by the College include the following: (1) Latin, Greek; (2) Spanish, Russian, German, French; (3) Mandarin, Modern Standard Hindi, Japanese, Farsi, Swahili, Indonesian, Arabic. All students are to learn one language from the last category to full spoken fluency and to at least a useful written serviceability, this to be accomplished in part by every student's spending a long term (normally the first term of Year III) in a country where the language is spoken. And I want all students, also, to learn to a fluency both spoken *and* written at least one language to be selected from the first two categories. I urge trustees and our first faculty to consider various means of facilitating the learning of these languages while the students are on the demesne. There are many: temporary assignments to language houses in interims, prolonged residences of guest professors from the various countries, the fullest use of all Internet resources, and so on. The argument that the average American student cannot possibly "do" such things is nonsense. If he wants to, he will.

Last, I have noted the extent to which the various subjects in the College's curriculum serve and complement each other. Perhaps none more usefully serves the interests of our country, in its life among the competing sovereignties of the world's community of nations. To know the mind of our friend and of our adversary, we must know his language, just as we will understand best those factors which helped form and condition our *own* political culture by learning the languages in which its antecedents were born, and in which they grew to a certain maturity—Greek and Latin.

Mathematics

Among the curious intellectual legacies of the nineteenth century is the notion, by now hardened into a psychosis for many, that the understanding of mathematics requires a "gift," and that this gift is but randomly vouchsafed to common humanity, and is but rarely bestowed upon girls and women.

In earnest and well-intentioned propitiation of those who believe themselves deprived of such a gift, our universities for some time have offered mathematical tuition in the spirit of Calculus for the Common Man, Easy Listenin' to Numbers 'n' Things, Mathematics for the Liberal Artist, and so on. More and more, such schools dismiss the requirement altogether for those who do not want to enroll in courses for which they imagine themselves to be overmatched.

All of which constitutes an insult to girls, women, and indeed the young men who, left to their own devices, would avoid taking courses in mathematics. No way of proceeding is better calculated to achieve the outcome it deserves than this.

The College's fixed curriculum should require two full terms of mathematics, possibly a third (I leave that for the first board and faculty to determine). The courses should be taught by mentors and professors who have proved themselves as teachers with a particular bent for effective teaching of undergraduates, and who will not be disheartened that their pupils may be slower in mathematics than themselves. For much of their early work, alas, will surely be by way of remediation: of undoing the damage done to too many of our early cohorts by high school mathematics courses (or requirements) like those I have mentioned.

Most entering students will be ill-prepared for college calculus. Our first mathematics course will have to address weak backgrounds, if any, in trigonometry; in function terminology, graphs of functions and equations, and probably too such things as inequalities of absolute values, parenthesization of expressions, factoring by distribution; and finally analytic trigonometry. Members of Cohort I must be known to have mastered a reasonable definition of the term "function" and to be able to describe the range and domain of a simple algebraic function, its principal branches, and the computation of their inverses.

As for calculus, it is inconceivable to me that an American college student in the year 2000 and beyond should not have learned to work comfortably through problems in single-variable calculus, series and functions of several variables, and other topics offered in conventional courses in integral calculus. I may be taxing your patience, Robert, if not your understanding, but our students must learn to apply differential calculus both to other mathematical topics and to physical, real-world problems.

The second half of the calculus sequence will comprise both series calculus and the calculus of several variables—and with them a presentation of some of the more basic methods of differential equations. I am talking specifically of such things as the convergence properties of power series, with augmentation by more traditional considerations related both to extension of Taylor's polynomial to Taylor's series and "to the uniqueness," as a colleague puts it, "of power series representations of functions." As for differential equations, our coverage should probably extend to the minimum, at least, capable of supporting the work we will require, again of all students, in elementary physics.

As you can see, Robert, I have kept my oar moving through the water, in mathematics as well as philosophy and history. And I hope you have, too. Have you? Or have you passively acquiesced in your daughter's reassurance that she should not "take math in college" because she does not "need" it, and because, later on, you can get someone to do that for you?

Logic

Herndon said of Abraham Lincoln: "All his great qualities were swayed by the *despotism of his logic*." It is a despotism fundamental to the ability to give useful service in the arts of citizenship and leading.

Verbal facility, easy assurance in utterance and elocution, an authoritative tone, and a yeasty stock of miscellaneous information (we dare not call it knowledge) make the image but not the fact of what America calls a smart person. Unfortunately the same citizen is rarely wise. He has rarely thought hard about the premises of his opinions or the architecture of his judgments. In his political usages he shouts out, after the vulgar fashion of the day, "sentences that he has never thought," rodomontade and partisan imprecation less calculated to expose the truth than to cement political advantage or interest, or to demonstrate orthodoxy and loyalty to party.

If our graduates are to be deliberate and intelligent practitioners of the arts and duties of citizenship, all after their own fashion, they must be trained to think logically. The College should therefore insist on a course in Logic, and I think it should be offered by our mathematicians. Students need to be made to consider seriously the tools and structures of verbal communication. They need to be schooled to use words that "say" what they are intended to communicate. Such a course should comprise symbolic and modern logic both: the former because, as has been accurately said, it "allows the form and structure of a statement to be divorced entirely from its colloquial meanings and implications"; and the latter because of its implications for a world of communication in which machine intelligences are growing, virtually each day, more seductive and potent.

Science

Courses in (1) geology and environment and (2) physics should be required. The necessity for the former seems to be self-evident. Within the compass of the College's boundaries lies a vast outdoor laboratory for the study of geology, not excluding the fossil legacies of a vast prehistoric sea to our immediate east. As to the environment, plainly it must be considered in a way I would call (it is the curse of the age that I must call it) prepolitical. Earlier we noted that merely to raise a *question* about race was, in some minds, equivalent to disqualifying the questioner as a participant in the ensuing discussion, since, by posing the question, he had declared an implicit bias. I am afraid that, at this writing, the "environment" is near to provoking an equivalent, and equivalently disqualifying, giddiness and intemperance—i.e., to propose a study of the environment is to invite censure as a "liberal."

O judgment, thou art fled to brutish beasts!

I note that the rising generation, universally almost, does not consider the matter in any way "political."

As to physics, I forbear to place the course in any sequence, except to say that physics should not be offered before our required mathematics courses.

Our study should embrace essential tenets of Newtonian mechanics and classical electrodynamics both. Our laboratories should have the best equipment possible, but in this instance I want no piece of apparatus attached to a computer. I do not want them learning—here—to manipulate computers. For correlation of data derived from experiments, yes; but not *for* the experiments themselves.

Latterly the program should comprise the subjects most colleges call modern physics. We should remember that the transition from the classical Newtonian world to the Nuclear Age was made in less than seventy years. Here, I am afraid that lectures and seminars, and some individual tuition, must supplant the work of the laboratory; students would learn little from simply duplicating the experiments of this age, and indeed little experimental work of this magnitude could be duplicated in our laboratories. Meantime an acute understanding of the fundamental discoveries of the period *is* possible, given our students' mathematical resources by this time: Einstein's Special Theory of Relativity; Particle Wave Duality; Quantum Mechanics and the Schrodinger Equation; and, finally, Nuclear Reactions with special emphasis on its applications. I am afraid that a rich understanding of such topics cannot come from a mere duplication of original experiments, but rather it comes from the manipulation of the various building block formulae produced by these experiments.

The College should require one additional science course. This course, in the history of science, will concentrate on the achievements (and how they were wrought) of the giants of science: Copernicus, Galileo, Newton, Darwin, Einstein. The achievements of each should be fitted into the context of their debts to their predecessors as well as the attacks of their critics. When you studied history at Chicago, Robert, you must have been given "review articles" from British journals. This is what I mean: a review article considers a new, important book; it salutes the work in the first paragraph, and then presents a brisk history of *earlier* considerations of the subject the new book is about. Each is set, that is to say, contextually and historically. I think the achievements of each scientist should be pondered—studied—also in terms of their cultural effects and implications. Such a course would allow time, also, for study and analysis of the major inventions of the twentieth century, not excluding (if I may be forgiven) the antecedents and development of the microprocessor.

Philosophy, Theology, Deontology

The College must offer instruction in the history of philosophy; in ethics; in comparative religions; in both the Old and

New Testaments of the Bible and in what Dr. Bellah has called the American "Civil Religion"; in fundamental issues of theology, not excluding that of theodicy; and, finally, in what we may call *deontology*, from the Greek *deon*—that which is proper and needful: *doing what is right.*

The last is of peculiar importance to our College and mission. I do not prescribe how it should be taught, but I intend that it be a foundation for a lifetime's consideration of how each graduate should *live* his life—so far as that life touches and is touched by the responsibilities and obligations of an active American citizen. This in turn implies a continual consideration of how we compose and conduct our own lives. I would offer the deontology course (program seminar, tutorial) during the second year of the five-year course. It would fit particularly well here, it seems to me, given that Cohort II is shortly to leave the College for its term of language study, and living in a foreign culture lends itself aptly for the consideration of the issues implied. And the central "issue," simply, is "How Should I Live?"

I am troubled profoundly by the current adduction of large religions as mere confirmators of *The Way I Want to Live*: that is, as a man who lays up treasures on earth, and who is, not infrequently, a son of a bitch to everyone around him. In what way, that is to ask, can a man's faith make him a better secular man and a better citizen? Many pages ago I took issue with Cardinal Newman. I do so again.

The deontology course would offer texts like the following: Socrates' *Apology*; *The Enchiridion* of Epictetus; Aristotle's *Ethics*; *The Meditations* of Marcus Aurelius; the *Analects* of Confucius; *The Imitation of Christ* by Thomas à Kempis; Cicero's *On Duties*; but also such things as the *Jefferson Bible*; certain sections of

Huckleberry Finn; Reinhold Niebuhr's transcending *Moral Man and Immoral Society*; Henry James's *The Lesson of the Master*; the last page of *Middlemarch*; the *Autobiography of Benjamin Franklin*; Lord Chesterfield's *Letters* to his son; the Code of Conduct of the American soldier; Victor Frankl's *Man's Search for Meaning*.

Again, I urge that such texts be eked out, be buttressed, by examinations of how historical and contemporary figures have tried to meet and master the crises of their own lives—crises that oppose, or seem to pit, obligation versus conscience; duty versus family; and so on. The faculty should develop lists of noble lives: not so different in spirit from those of Plutarch, except that they should be lives of men and women of the nineteenth and twentieth centuries, lives whose authors we can "realize," in ways that, perhaps, we cannot with Tacitus, the Younger Cato, Pericles, and the other great heroes of antiquity. An individual life studied, known, loved (the love strengthened by our knowledge of its dark corners and failures as well as the titles it furnishes to greatness) is a more potent, more lasting illumination and fuel for our own, than an intellectual ability to consider issues of ethics in the abstract—however valuable. That our fellow citizens of 1998 are but titillated and distracted by the sexual scandals, real or alleged, in Washington—and not, as Americans, appalled by them, outraged and ashamed—is the grim, inescapable proof of what our age has become.

Matthew Arnold reminds us that "moral rules, apprehended as ideas first, and then rigorously followed as laws, are, and must be, for the sage only. The mass of mankind can be carried along a course full of hardship for the natural man, can be borne over the thousand impediments of the narrow way, *only by the tide of a joyful and binding emotion.*" The likelihood of our learning to live nobler, better lives is increased, in proportion as we are touched, in our emotion, as we listen with the ear of the heart, to the legacies and lessons of individual lives we know of, and cherish.

Composition/Rhetoric

Fifty years ago Lionel Trilling said that philosophical conservatism had become little more than a series of "irritable mental gestures." I do not know if that was true; it is not so today. But the phrase is serviceable, and contemporary American political discourse *is* conducted in irritable mental gestures or scripted, inglorious buncombe, weltering phrases in search of an organizing idea (as someone wrote of Harding's speeches). These gestures are the verbal resources of a people perpetually tired; who do not know what they mean, though they know what they want; who lack the resources to communicate what they want; who have somehow (I know not how) lost their willingness to speak directly and plainly; whose own education has ignored good books, good speeches—good writing; who have no contemporary models; and whose culture both incubates the practice of insincerity and discourages pith. Pith can hurt; and we must strike glancing blows, not direct hits. *Kindly, therefore, extinguish all smoking materials while you discuss enhancing revenues.* Here we see plainly the direct link between "character" and communication: the person of strong and honorable character being predisposed to say exactly what he means, without apology or euphemism.

An accurate pen must precede a fluent one. We resist for the moment the implications of the ethernet in choosing our metaphors. We have to make certain our pupils know how to compose ordinary English sentences of accurate words accurately arranged. This implies remedial instruction, probably, between the time of their acceptance and the time of their arrival for their first orientation month—and probably more such instruction beyond that time. I do not presume to suggest, much less dictate, how such instruction should be rendered. I am a partisan, however, of models. Read good prose all the time, and you are bound to learn something that will help you write, and speak, more accurately, more usefully, yourself. Emulation here is as valuable as emulation in other aspects of our kind of education. Degas wrote, in another context altogether: "The masters must be copied over and over again: and it is only after proving yourself a good copyist that you should reasonably be permitted to draw a radish from nature." I am not certain why this should not be so for young people who want, or need, to learn how to write.

The young should be given models of simple, lucid prose to study and learn to emulate. Simple prose, graceful and accurate in its conveyance of its writer's exact intent. Pupils should and can read such prose when very young. It is not the prose of "textbooks," but the prose of Jane Austen or E.B. White, of Macaulay, of Alexandre Dumas, Mikhail Lermontov, James Madison. In the same way a child should be taught to play the piano, for example: not by learning the watery fomentations of music educationists, but the simplest primary melodies of Mozart, Beethoven, Schumann, Bartok.

I believe also that no one being taught to write should be excused from the requirement of describing things, and in a detailed, accurate, exhaustive catalogue of exactitude. We should place before our students therefore models of exemplary prose, for our purpose prose selected for its clarity and simplicity. Such models are found in the best literatures in the world; only rarely in contemporary political discourse.

Toward the end of these notes I shall have something to say about *memorization*: the ultimate means of "inculcating" a sense of what is choice, exquisite, "classical," in writing. Memorization, of course, has no part in contemporary education; the age is hostile to this, too.

All students must be made to begin the habit, on arrival at the demesne, of keeping daily journals and commonplace books: the former at least in part catalogues of exactitude, not unlike those maintained by the poet Hopkins, in which he *tried*, disciplined himself to render in prose precisely what it was he saw. Again: our mission is not to train up writers and scholars, but public people and leaders; these most urgently need to know how to communicate accurately, and must have schooled their eyes and their pens to find and record the singular, the out-of-the-way, the disregarded, the individual thing or person or gesture. We think of Lincoln as our greatest presidential writer. He was, beyond question. His speeches and letters fuse the exalted, the visionary sentiments of a great man with those of the humblest and most arresting details, never unnoticed: rather laid up for later, and telling us.

As to "public speaking," which (I have read) is more terrifying to Americans than death or cobras, *we can make every student at the College an effective orator, and it is a critical feature of our mission.* The way to do this is simply to require students to "speak" in such circumstances often, to offer steady criticism of such speaking whatever the venue, to insist that they learn such skill in part by reading the best political/public speeches that our Western history has to offer us, and to get into their characters the habit of insisting on preparing and writing their own speeches. Who else, you may ask, would write a college sophomore's speech? That is not my point. My point is that we must develop in our students such an avid interest in doing this thing for themselves—call it pride of authorship if you will—that they will never want or seek to delegate the duty when they are leaders, in business, in government, or wherever their ambitions lead them.

We should inculcate a positive aversion from motivational harangues—either rendering or receiving such factitious froth, concocted only to line the pocket of the speaker, or befog the brain of the listener, or both. Students should be made to speak at many venues: at refectory meals, all–College assemblies, chapels, lectures, and classes.

The quality of public speaking in our country, and in the West generally, is illimitably debased. There are two reasons for this. The first is that we do not educate our young people to communicate correctly for *any* purpose. The second is that the fundamental requisite for effectual public communication is character, and character cannot be counterfeited. A staple of character is honesty: this means writing and saying what we think (a duty that we cannot ordinarily "delegate" to an aide, an assistant, or a writer of speeches). Aristotle understood this well. Character is the essential coherence of a man's virtues, and his words are an artifact of his integrity. When we say that George Marshall could go before congressional committees during World War II and be certain that everything he said *would be taken as the earnest and objective assessment and counsel of a man motivated only by a perfect passion for the public good*, we are close to what Aristotle meant, and what we must still mean. Our American people know and understand good character when they see and hear it. It remains the most precious resource of any public person seeking office or determined to render any service to the Republic.

There is a datum, Robert, that you will surely cite in refutation: that is, the poll number that purports to demonstrate that, although the "public" is disappointed in the character of its highest leadership, it nonetheless is "satisfied" with such leadership, because... and here bromides are concocted and served, their burden being that things "are pretty good," the economy is healthy, and other such blather. For a while such dissonance can exist, but not for long. For the character of a public man or woman cannot be hidden or disguised, and history—as with JFK—will have its revenge.

Imaginative Literature

I have put "5%" alongside this heading. Two courses, you may infer. I am diffident about doing this. I am not a student of literature; I am a reader of books, and my appetite is much better described as voracious than discriminating.

Here the College's interest lies in creating a passion for reading. When I say imaginative literature I mean prose fiction—novels, stories, plays, poetry, criticism of a certain kind, essays. I urge no argument, only the honest conviction that, excepting life itself, it has been imaginative literature that has taught me what I have most craved to know, and needed to know of women and men, that has taught me those things that I now see I could scarcely have lived without.

I inflict no gushing apologia, rather set down several small acknowledgments of gifts of letters to my own life:

The last paragraph of *Middlemarch*, the essence of what the nineteenth century has to teach our College. Radiant and calm in its quiet summary of what charged experience has infused into a small, blameless, disregarded life; and has taught it while that life has yet many years left unto it. It is balm to my own life, here on its trackless final margins, just as it may be a sustaining inspiration to all who labor in the thought that life obliges them to find glory, authority, fame, power.

"Sonnet XXIX," Shakespeare.

The great speeches in *Julius Caesar* and *Henry V* (I might inflict huge lists of such speeches, from most of the plays, but to what end?): from which I have learned, in such a way as never to forget, that "the abuse of greatness is when it disjoins remorse from power," a lesson that anyone who leads or presumes to train himself to lead must carry in his bones. Leaders must share and suffer before they can presume to lead and direct.

The Charterhouse of Parma: in which Stendahl taught me what I had lived through but not learned on Iwo Jima, and taught me in a way that no philosopher or historian, theologian or anthropologist could ever hope to do—and taught me in a way that flung me forward into the poetry of Wilfred Owen and back into Tolstoy, and the huge family of the Russian writers from Pushkin forward.

We have observed already that, in our obligation to learn the characters of those countries with whom we will strive or ally, or of those whom we will have to fight, we must know their souls and their heritages, their gods and their virtues—and we will find them in their literatures before we find them in their economics and politics. All our students must devote significant parts of their terms abroad reading in the *literatures* of the countries to which we send them.

We cannot measure the effects of a lifetime's quiet reading of such literatures upon the sensibilities and judgments of public men and women, men and women who must *act, direct, lead, decide*. Yet it seems irrefutable that their judgments are bound to be more complete, less solipsistic, more compassionate, ultimately more accurate than those who do not read the literature of the imagination. We cannot prove this, Robert, but we know it.

Again, I do not prescribe, but I suggest courses in American literature; in Shakespeare; in the literature of Russia and of that country to which our student is assigned on his language interim; and, finally, in private studies in the literature of Attic Greece and of late Republican Rome, and the Rome of Augustus.

Make them read things whole, and with their commonplace books at the ready. Do not get anthologies or excerpts.

Mentors and professors of imaginative literature should always include writers of fiction, poets, essayists—creators and practitioners of an art of which the rest of us are but critics or humbly grateful beneficiaries.

Students with the vocation and perhaps the requisite talent should be encouraged to write—and recite—poetry and prose fiction at refectory reading times.

Fine Arts at the College

I write from the perspective of an American disappointed at the dry meagerness of his contemporaries' interests and cultivated sensibilities, not to say, their knowledge and enthusiasm for painting, music, sculpture, opera, and the arts generally. It is not a matter of their want of what an earlier time called extracurricular culture. It is a matter of their having missed the frail opportunity a certain education might somehow have laid before them, one that might have disclosed an avocation of the kind that demands to be sustained by hearing and seeing gifted artists. Joy, refreshment, wonder, imaginative resourcefulness—

all denied generations of twentieth-century Americans, most particularly denied public people and businessmen, it seems to me. They do not read, they have no literature, their public pronouncements are mere functional jointures of wonkism unenlivened by the wit, the pungency, the singing or visual metaphors that an earned culture—one "earned" by avocation—might have brought them. All they say and write conveys but a weary purposiveness; their leisure, so far from being used as a time of refreshment in such ways, is embraced merely as a period to sit in one of those sunlit hells of boredom about which the critic wrote, there to consider one's finances, homes, travel arrangements, medicines, servants, and dinner partners. We are a generation of CEOs that knows not Mozart, Bach, Schumann; van Eyck, Degas, Bosch; and that, when it thinks of a "classic," thinks of an old edition, thrown into an attic garret in a summer residence, of *The House of the Seven Gables*. It is particularly lamentable that it knows not its own country's heritage of art and music.

The famous John Adams famously wrote, "I must study politics and war, that my sons may have liberty to study mathematics and philosophy. My sons ought to study mathematics and philosophy, geography, natural history, and naval architecture, in order to give their children a right to study painting, poetry, music, architecture, statuary, tapestry, and porcelain...."

It is a lovely formulation, and among all the *obiter dicta* of a jammed and diffuse life, most urgently craves remembering. The twenty-first century rememberer should bear in mind that the studies Adams prescribes for succeeding generations are not mutually exclusive—i.e., he has no expectation that the third generation's leisure (earned by its predecessors) to study painting, poetry, music, and so on, will mean that it no longer has to study war and politics. On the contrary, it will be obliged—but privileged—to do both.

While he was writing Marlborough's *Life*, Winston Churchill painted many gay canvases, brooded over his country's willful descent from military strength, served in the House of Commons, recited great hearty chunks of poetry, and wrote brilliant occasional journalism. The intellectual and spiritual nourishments of his long life seemed to proclaim that, not only can we have war and politics, and statuary, painting, and poetry at the same time, *we had better have them at the same time.*

Our school should be an enterprise saturated in the fine arts—as a living and enduringly worthwhile enterprise that is neither a refuge, nor a social crutch, nor a home for pretense. Every student should be given a course in painting—should be taught to paint. Every student should enroll in art history, and we should insist that every student learn the art of the country to which he is sent for his language term. And although I plan on leaving my own collection to the College, most of it to be housed, I suppose, in a gallery, I insist that the College's collections also be displayed in places where, invariably, most colleges do not display their collections. In places where lovely paintings pop up unexpectedly, in the gym foyer or the office on the second floor of the science building. Art should be integrated into our lives, not seen as an escape from them, and therefore not isolated in gallery warehouses.

A colleague, W.A. Badgett, quotes the composer George Rochberg's reaction to an all-Stravinsky concert many years ago:

I was exhilarated and my ears were ringing with the *klang* of his new music—with new and revitalized incisiveness and clarity... and so full of the sense of vitality and well-being... for the first time in my life I felt I was inside his music. Its oddly asymmetric shapes, its vibrant, gorgeous colors, its strangely personal song emerge with utter clarity and directness... the whole impression was one of radiance—of spirit and intelligence, energy, and verve.

I want the College also to offer a course, one or two terms, in the history of Western music; to retain musicians for various residences during the year; to sponsor a musical competition in the summers on the demesne for pianists; and to insist (like St. John's College in Annapolis) that each student learn to read musical notation and to play, however rudimentarily, an instrument. I intend to purchase grand pianos for the refectories of each village, and upright pianos for the parlors of each house.

Some years ago I heard the Mozart Triple Piano Concerto, one of whose soloists was Helmut Schmidt, then chancellor of Germany. The next morning Schmidt appeared on a televised news interview in Washington, answering questions in clearer, more engaging English than that of his interlocutors. He wore his cultivation so lightly and so effortlessly, and I remember thinking that somehow each of his vocations in some way helped enrich and sustain the vitality of the others.

I cited Thucydides: if a man has no public business, then we say he has no business at all. We might also say (because it *must* be said of our trashy political culture in 1998) that if a man has no private intellectual "business," if his aesthetic and intellectual capabilities become stunted and desiccated, then the quality of his public contribution must be diminished. He may have earned, through education and experience, the faculty of reliable and calm judgment, but surely it is his continuing engagement in the humane letters and the fine arts that can best sustain his capacity for wonder, that can preserve unjaded his responsiveness to the new and singular. We do not say he will embrace the new, but he will, always, be eager to learn, to understand. Wordsworth talked of the still, sad music of humanity. The political leader or general who no longer hears such music disserves both himself and his country. Some years ago I came across a line that lingers in the memory: "The successful general allows into his mind only neutral factors of calculation." I regard the formulation as both wrong and dangerous; it is appropriate for warlords, but not for leaders of the American Republic.

Atonement with the Machine

The College's five-year program provides four August orientation sessions. Sessions Two and Three should be devoted to teaching our students how to *do* practical and needful things.

Session Two—the first "Atonement with the Machine" session—would introduce members of Cohort II to the use of the most basic tools: screws, levers, inclined planes, level and square. It would move them to a basic mastery of modern tools, including woodworking devices, automotive tools (hammer, square, drill, plane), outdoor tools, and equipment shop tools like the lathe, band saw, and drill press. I also see our students building things: learning basic construction techniques comprising bricks and mortar, wood, electrical circuits, cabinetry, plumbing, roofing, well-digging, and the like; and the investigation of common building materials. Finally, the College might ask members of each village contingent in Cohort II actually to build some permanent device or structure for the College. Alternatively, a machine might be constructed using hand tools and technologies available to the original constructors of prototypes on which their evolved contemporary machines are based: clockworks, for example; lifting devices; and, for historical interest, such siege engines as the trebuchet and catapult.

You will note, Robert, my hostility to the evolved mode of living of our American clerisy, and my determination that, for our little College at least, it be thwarted before it can infect those we graduate, by making our pupils handy with tools that will enable them to "do" for themselves, just as, when they order men and women to war, it will be not only other men's daughters and sons who will have to go—but also ours. Indeed, that is why—I know, more controversially—I want our third August orientation to examine basic weapon systems, including the physics of their use and development; the consequences of their introduction into the operation of war; as well as the basic construction of jeeps and trucks, which could be built for the use of the College.

Students should study ballistics and properties of common explosives, and they should be trained in the use of firearms; the program should certify them as proficient in the use of a number of them. We will teach our students that, to paraphrase *Shane*, a weapon is a tool like any other, and no better and no worse than the man or woman behind it. Just as we impart other knowledges, so should we impart this. The chances that our graduates may find themselves in harm's way are in my judgment not receding but multiplying. They must be ready.

Orientation Month: The Computer

I leave it to the founding board and faculty to prepare a proper orientation, about a month in length I should think, for the new members of Cohort I. Clearly their translation from their homes to the demesne in the Laramies will be a radical one, and they will need to adjust themselves rapidly to our expectations for them—indeed, to a new way of living altogether. I should think the board can infer pretty well from what I have written what kinds of things an orientation will have to consider.

We must assume that by the end of orientation every student is usefully literate in uses of the computer, so that some sort of orientation curriculum here is essential. No member of Cohort I can begin his academic work in September without a comfortable facility in the use of a word processor, without an efficient skill in retrievals from the Internet and its associated facilities, or without skill in using spreadsheets.

But if that is what we must assume by the end of orientation, we can assume nothing of the kind at the beginning. The children of automated privilege, as my doctor calls it, are sophisticated almost beyond belief—but they will compose only a small number of our students. Most of our new pupils, certainly in the early days of the College, will be illiterate—literally—in all computer usages, and may never have used a computer at all. Even those who consider themselves reasonably proficient will have atrociously poor keyboarding skills.

So a crude syllabus based on an assumed lowest common denominator of computer proficiency should be prepared early; as this work is going forward, the board and faculty should do what they can to encourage, if they cannot require, all entering students to develop computer skills between the time of their selection for admission and their enrollment. Earlier I noted that we will give all students a laptop, which of course will help them develop computer skills; I somehow think I can prevail on the company to provide the computers in perpetuity.

Grades

You may recall that I mentioned there will be no grades.

The Israeli Army (so I've been told) does not give decorations for exemplary performance of duty. The message is plain: gravely to fulfill their obliged duties is simply what the nation's citizen soldiers are conscripted *for*; the inward satisfactions of knowing that they have fulfilled them is recompense enough.

I do not want grades given at the College. Rather, students should be rated as "proficient" or "not proficient" in their academic courses; nothing more. Remember that the relations between students and mentors, particularly those mentors assigned as principal mentors to each student, will be very close; through them the students will know with precision how well they're doing, and when they have done unusually admirable or unsatisfactory work. This is enough. The country is off its rocker on this business of grades. What are we to make of the fact that, while Scholastic Aptitude Test scores are dropping like an Otis elevator, the percentages of college students "getting" A's is rising like a rocket; and that vast numbers of high school students are carrying averages in excess of 4.0, the presumed peak of perfection?

Let us stay away from this buncombe.

A Few Comments on the Calendar and the Five-Year Cursus

First, with exceptions as noted, I do not presume to prescribe when each subject (or the courses into which it may be divided) is to be offered. Certain obvious requirements will suggest themselves to all: the need, for example, to assure fluent computer literacy early in our students' first year; and the prerequisite demands of composition, mathematics, and foreign languages. The framers of the curriculum must remember that Cohort III will be abroad for the first long term, studying the language spoken in the host country to which cohort members are assigned. Obviously some fluency in that language will be needed by the time each cohort leaves the College for its term abroad.

I urge trustees and early leaders of the College to consider how best, also, to "mix" various topics and courses. Earlier I suggested that painting be required in Term I, Year I; given the other requirements of that term, not to mention those of Trek, of learning to live and work in a new and somewhat alien environment, however lovely, it would seem a useful form of creative diversion as well as useful education. We remember what too much mathematics and political economy did to John Stuart Mill.

Alternating terms and interims, separated usually by vacations of ten days, makes sense to me. Ordinarily each student would take five courses each full term; one each interim that he spends on the demesne; three for the term he is abroad. (Remember that for two other interims he is to be doing his service requirement—nonmilitary—away from the College.) Year IV, for reasons I will detail, is to be spent entirely in military training and on active service: a time shorter than the traditional American conscript's obligated service, but the same as, or longer, than that of most Western countries at this turn of the twenty-first century.

I want all students to be on the demesne, together as a College, together in their villages, for the four-week orientation session each August. And when our students *do* leave us for their terms abroad and military years, they should leave together, *en bloc*, with fitting send-offs, affirmations of high purpose, times together, including a few days on Trek, before leaving.

As configured, the full five-year curriculum allows for about forty-three course periods: eleven or twelve each of the first two years, when all terms are spent at the College; nine during Year III; eleven during the final year.

A simple depiction of the College's annual calendar, configured for the five-year *cursus* of an entering student, is presented on the next page.

Orientation 4 weeks	MAJOR TERM 14 weeks	Christmas Vacation 2 weeks	Interim 6 weeks	Vacation 1 week	MAJOR TERM 14 weeks	Vacation 1 week	Interim 6 weeks	Summer Vacation 4 weeks
Opening Orientation Computer Mastery	5 Subjects/Term						Language Segment	
Atonement with the Machine			Service Internship					
Atonement with the Machine	Language Study Abroad						Service Internship	
		REQUIRED MILITARY SERVICE						

D<small>EAR</small> R<small>OBERT</small>,

I must discuss in more detail military service at the College. Our fourth-year cohort will serve on active duty as private soldiers in the Marines or the Army. That service will comprise the basic training common to all who enter either service; advanced individual training in one of its combat arms, such as the infantry; and an assignment of about six months with an infantry, armored, or Marine division, preferably one serving overseas. All members of the cohort will remain in reserve status following their return to the College for Year V, and for the normal reserve commitment of years after graduation. Some few of our alumni may wish to attain commissions and remain with the colors. I should say, too, that our young women will *not* be expected to serve in direct combat units. But they must do their service in the *military* establishment.

The burdens of defending our democratic Republic must be borne equitably, and when the supreme sacrifice is to be exacted—and it will be, again and again, because only the dead, the philosopher tells us, have seen the end of war—when this sacrifice is paid in the currency of blood, it must not be paid only by the poor, by the ill-educated, or by black men. All must be liable, and since I cannot hope to persuade my fellow countrymen of the wisdom of my judgment, I simply make military service a requirement for our pupils.

There are several compelling reasons for my insistence on this point. I have already stated the first. It is terrible enough when a young American, his future pure possibility, is killed fighting. It may be necessary, yes, but why should these young die, by reason of their ignorance as fresh-faced recruits, when old campaigners—lifetime practitioners of the soldier's art, patriots and experts who have *chosen* to make their lives in uniform—generally come through safe by reason of their skill.

War is terrible; and the deployments of American soldiers abroad have been coming thick and fast these last ten years— *accelerating, not declining*, in numbers of assignments since the end of the Soviet Union and the well-organized, brittlely stable Cold War. The trend will continue.

Oxford went into the trenches in 1914, as did the Sorbonne. But Harvard and Stanford did not patrol the rice paddies in 1968 or deploy to Kuwait in 1991. *When war comes, those to whom our culture has given the most, including those who have earned the most for themselves, should be as liable to serve in harm's way as those who have nothing*, or who have volunteered for military service because other opportunities seem less plausible. During the "sixties," or what we call the sixties (in reality what we call the sixties is the period from 1967 to 1974), American academia raged against the war; but theirs was an untested probity—they raged, but they were deferred from the draft. Other men's sons—from Mississippi and South Philadelphia and Newark— went into the Ia Trang Valley or the Parrot's Beak.

Since the beginning of 1973 there has been no draft, no conscription, so that the chasm is deeper and wider now than it was even then. I mean the chasm between the way the American clerisy looks at war and military service, and the way those who will fight, one day, must know it. When I say "clerisy," I mean the word in the old-fashioned, Victorian sense: the educated verbal class that comprises lawyers and publishers, professors, ministers, writers, lobbyists, bureaucrats, and journalists. Hardly any one of them under the age of, say, fifty, ever served or was even liable to be called up. Now they fill the offices of state in all their branches; some of them will send our children into harm's way, or pontificate about whether and how the children should or should not be more efficiently deployed, and so on, waving their hands over large-scale maps while our sons crawl forward three feet in a swamp.

Two or three years ago I heard a speech by a young woman who had organized some sort of national teaching volunteer corps, recruiting from famous colleges in the East that have glittering *cachet*. The new graduates would teach in difficult circumstances, in disregarded villages in the hardscrabble rural South or in troubled urban neighborhoods, for meager salaries. Someone asked her, do you expect these bright young people will *remain* in teaching? No, she said. But in fifteen or twenty years they will serve on school boards and they will understand what we ask teachers to do.

I believe our clerisy, specifically those elected or appointed to high federal offices, need to understand what they will call upon young soldiers to "do." *The abuse of greatness is when it disjoins remorse from power.* It has never been written better.

I come to a second reason.

The large novels of the 1939–1945 war, hawked in their paperback incarnations by the adjective "sprawling," seemed always to fasten upon small groups of American soldiers whom circumstance had flung together, usually for training as well as for fighting. Such groups embraced Jews, Episcopalians, black men, southerners, lumberjacks, intellectuals, ploughboys, Romeos, and so on. Usually a southern NCO was set over them; or a bitter professional soldier, thirty-five or forty, who had washed up on the sunless shore of the regular army in the Depression. All subsisted uneasily together, until some incident fused them, made them see each other for what each man was, stripped of his accent or his wallet. When the war ended, each returned to his city or his farm a far, far better man: particularly so, for the purposes of our Republic, for purposes of citizenship and understanding how things work. The picture is an idealized one, no doubt; and the war they fought elicited the kind of national response whose passion inspired most who served—on Omaha Beach, flying the Hump, even in a training depot on the Great Plains. Military service as an instrument of a certain kind of socialization is unexcelled: making people in groups do what they would just as soon not do, provided what you make them do is lawful, is as valuable to them as it is important to the Republic.

Men of my generation retain a perhaps puzzling affection for the military services—in my own case, for the Marines— an affection puzzling if not troubling to our grandchildren. It helps explain my own insistence on our students' military service. What John Houseman used to pronounce in those Smith Barney ads might be transmuted to a potent endorsement of the cardinal reason for serving: we merited our citizenship the old-fashioned way... we *earned it*—on Iwo Jima, at Anzio, and over Ploesti. We thought of no such thing at the time; but I do now. I also believe that a year or two of military service and training at the entry level is simply good for our citizens. It is a good thing for young persons to have to execute orders with which they may not agree, or whose requirements they'd just as soon avoid, not excluding all the military adiaphora (things seemingly of no consequence)—the obsessive sweeping and painting, cleaning, dropping for push-ups, and being awakened at four, in January, for a two-mile run. It is a good thing also, more importantly, to know that one is liable to be placed in harm's way at any moment for a noble cause—and serving the Republic is always noble—particularly for a generation that believes an antibiotic or an orthopedic surgeon can swiftly fix anything that bedevils it.

These Americans who grow up in gated communities (I think they are called), who swank and beaver their way through country day schools, and both serve and assuage their parents' insecurities by playing certain sports and instruments and enrolling in certain universities and joining certain clubs and professions, and never knowing our country or its polyglot people, or never having to risk and sacrifice in trades that may soil their hands or impede their ascents—these are our countrymen who *need* what that large war forced upon us. (Incidentally, we do not deter war by shrinking our forces to half their Cold War strength, or by forcing them to make do with weapons from the second worst decade of this century—the seventies. I would immediately reinstitute the draft, by lottery, no exemptions.)

Mr. George Kennan notes the native American suspicion of elites. But the elite that he cherishes and that our College must exemplify, and champion, is—as he says—an eliteness of opportunity honestly earned and exploited, and of service to the Republic. The *sacramentum* that will bind our pupils to their obligation, a vow that commits them as surely as the vow of a priest must confirm his allegiance to his calling—that *sacramentum* insists on the immersion of ego, will, personal desire, in the necessary work of causes we may not "like." But I expect our students, at the College, during their service, and in their long careers afterwards, to learn to subsume ego in larger purposes, and to do it without regret, remorse, or cavil; and to efface so far as it is possible the whispered urgings of rapacious ego. They must learn to work not for celebrity or power or material reward, but to satisfy the needs of community and country. If fame is the last infirmity of the noble mind, let them understand that the only fame worth the achievement is the fame that comes unsought, or that is given our name after we are gone.

Finally: solders destroy things. As medical doctors may inflict pain to cultivate and sustain cure, soldiers may destroy to serve the defined interests and security of our country; ultimately to achieve a just peace, as that peace is earned by the effort they are obliged, by our elected government, to make. Ruskin once made a speech in which he insisted soldiers learn the value of what they may be called upon to destroy. Those who will one day lead our country must know the value of those they may order into battle. It is one thing to read sentimental speeches on Decoration Day, speeches prepared by members of political staffs, about brave lads; it is another, and better, thing that those who may, in the course of their duties, make such speeches know intimately and from experience who those young men are, and the costs of *their* destruction.

As ever,
John Adams

My dear Robert,

I am now the beneficiary of Voice Typing, installed by an old Carswell buddy two days ago, and probably not a day too soon, as I've got a hunch. My pain is obliterated; and there is a floating emptiness, not so much blessed as odd, in my spine and all along my left shoulder and collarbone, where the disease, well diffused, has taken up permanent housekeeping. It has brought all its family into all the rooms of the house; and they are drinking, fighting, lusting, screaming—and I can neither hear, nor feel, their pain. I am become the physical analogue, physical only, to Wordsworth's blessed mood, my *body* now the silence that is in the starry sky, the sleep that is among the lonely hills. I am reversing, that is to say, the metaphor: my body is at great and icy peace; my mind fuddled and foggy. I may not see these sentences (A passion-driven exultant man sings out/sentences that he has never thought) in hard copy; are they freight-train assemblies, Jamesian enjambments, strange slippery ragings at the dying of the light? Again: I look at my table, two feet from my face, and see the familiar forest of orange translucence, the silos of medicines and easeful surcease, for when you haven't got time for the pain. And here, it would appear, I haven't got time for anything.

The last section is simply "Who Will Lead Them?" and here I mean teachers as well as those who will help administer the school and, as a lawyer might say, actually lead it. I have made the cardinal distinction between those I call mentors and those who are professors; I disclose what I think should be the duties of each; I discuss also "administration" (when I think of administration I think of Lord Curzon, English viceroy of India), the president, and the board of trustees, and their various duties.

What is most important is our "mentors," these teacher-scholar-leaders, most of them pretty young I would hope, all of them men and women of *action* who love to teach and who have the kind of temperament that will, after they have fallen in love with our school, be its fierce, zealous partisans in all things. You have to go out and find them, Robert. A bunch of resumés tumbling over the transom or off the Net won't get it. Simply because credentials have little use or meaning for these positions. You will see what I mean.

My mind is all over the map, these things I am taking, and with some form of Metrecal like what they gave Christina, a long, long time ago. I somehow expect I will see her, as another poet said, on the edge of dust, "and know her as a faithful vestige must." What will she think of me? She will be, still, twenty-six, so inestimably lovely and so blameless… that is why I put the theodicy into the curriculum; Cohort III will make the aptest pupils for it, right, perhaps, after their return from learning Hindi and Russian, and from perhaps having seen how people live who were brought into being in the filth and squalor of Calcutta. I don't want it taught by some simpering defrocked academicky Person of God, either. I understand the bottom line is Suck It Up and do what you can, and quit worrying about it, as I must do.

We now have the incongruity of the Saint-Saens G-Minor Piano Concerto, the raffish bouncy Second Movement. Who put *that* on? It is automated, it happens at 4:30, like Ferris Bueller's answering machine responding to a call. You had expected the Mozart Requiem for me? or the Fauré? I don't know who put it on, and I don't want Saint-Saens in the musical *cursus*. For bouncy affirmation remain with your Mendelssohn, who also went early.

Last night I watched a review of Eisenhower's life and service. It ended with a voice-over quoting what were supposed to be his last words: I've always loved my wife, I've always loved my children, I've always loved my grandchildren, I've always loved my country. I do not know if he said such things, but I have always loved him and have felt myself drawn to him as the (what Emerson called Lincoln) quite native, aboriginal American— of our dying century, at least. Think about why this should be, Robert—I haven't got time: for the pain, now again, in the spine. Nelson, Stonewall Jackson, Caesar, Marcus Aurelius; I believe in what they are reported to have said when they died.

I can't talk much more for now. Who was it who said, My country, how I leave my country? Do you, can you, believe these things about the president? And that, it seems, it makes not a tinker's dam to anyone? This place and seat of honor, of another Adams, two of them, of Lincoln, TR, Wilson? It is a measure of what we are become. He is, so I am told, us.

In any case, the numbers are fine, and then some.

Your affectionate friend,
John Adams

*D*EAR MR. ADAMS,

Thank you for your letter—actually, I have an encouraging note about you from Dr. deBurgh, who says that getting slightly "cloudy" from morphine derivatives is metaphorical, not medical; that you were just tired. I like doctors, but they don't have much humor. He scolds you for sitting in the sun—there is the possibility of squamous cell skin cancer. Meantime you are on morphine-based medication for the malignancy that has spread from your prostate to your spine. I trust you don't mind my finding grim mirth in your physician's lack of it. But he does think your chances of remission, possibly full remission, are not insignificant.

I have approached two other men to serve as trustees; I have already sought and gained the assent of the board to add them, and I am confident that they will join us. One is Mathew Reardon, formerly of Bechtel and now chairman of the Casper construction company that bears his name. He will be a huge help to us. He understands conflict of interest. He knows the governor well. The other (I told you on the phone) is the head of the Virginia Military Institute—who is, I believe, a partisan of some of your notions of how to educate men, and now, I see, women. The full board will meet in May. It is reasonable to assume that we will be able to assemble all the planners, architects, builders, lawyers, and the rest, soon thereafter—and that we might break ground as early as the summer of this year, which would mean we could open in the fall of 2000. I will spare you the word millennium.

The Carswell Division of CPU (you saw the correspondence) is honored to commit to the notebook computers for every entering student and for all faculty, the latter to receive the latest model every two years.

You will forgive my mentioning that my daughter Ashley was accepted yesterday at Brown, where they have no required curriculum and where boys and girls live together in dormitories, and where such notions as those you propound would land you, well, I'm not sure where. But it is a great teaching school.

I trust this finds you improving every day, and sitting out in the sun, working on your tan.

Faithfully,
Robert Parkman

CHAPTER 6

Who Should Lead Them?

An outstanding personality can still triumph over that blind antipathy to virtue which is the defect of all states, small and great alike... he had the rare faculty of being familiar without weakening his authority and austere without forfeiting people's affection. To mention incorruptibility and strict honesty in a man of his calibre would be to insult his virtues.

Tacitus, *Agricola* IX

...as may lead and draw them in willing obedience, inflamed with the study of learning and admiration of virtue—stirred up with high hopes of living to be brave men and worthy patriots, dear to God and famous to all ages... [their teacher] with mild and effectual persuasions and what with the intimation of some fear, if need be, but chiefly by his own example, might in a short space gain them an incredible diligence and courage, infusing into their young breasts such an ingenuous and noble ardor....

Milton, *Of Education* (1644)

WHO SHOULD LEAD THEM?

This is the most important—and difficult—part of our work. Those we wish to hold up as examples to be emulated cannot be men and women who themselves fall far short of the ideals they propound.

We want to retain therefore honorable men and women who have answered an unignorable vocation to teach and serve the young: both by what they know and believe, and by how they live their lives. We want persons passionately devoted to the pursuit and propagation of truth wherever it leads them, and who are loyal to our students and the mission of the College.

In one of the unsung and almost unknown verses of "America, the Beautiful" there is the line "America, America, God mend thine ev'ry flaw." It is an exhortation, a plea, that as a people we remain constant and faithful to our founding creeds. Our leaders at the College, especially those who will inaugurate the work, oversee its construction and development, the preparation of its curriculum, its long orientation for our first cadre of mentors and professors both, the animation of the enterprise—they will determine whether the experiment fails or succeeds.

I use the word "lead" to connote the obligations of all the adults who are retained to work at the College—not only those few in positions of executive responsibility. I mean the president and his few associates, but also all teachers, and all the rest who will serve to make the venture successful. For all in some sense will lead, even those who are normally disregarded by clever students and learned professors: members of service offices, classified employees, buildings and grounds people, security officers and clerks. In many ways their leadership will be as important as that of our teachers.

Earlier I emphasized that such commitments as these do not imply a political homogeneity or an institutional orthodoxy of temperament, appearance, opinion, and such. The point deserves to be stressed. Our faculty will be united as patriots, of course; and as those who love to teach; and as those we can trust to live lives exemplary to the young students all around them. Beyond this, so far from trying to find teachers all cut from the same cloth, we should *positively seek out those whose lives and careers to date seem to have made them fiercely independent, strong-minded "characters" of the sort in which the young delight, and from whom they are likely to learn the most.* The young love vivid, outspoken teachers, not cautious calculators of the effects they are making or of the risks they are running. I want men and women like that.

A dead scholar in the Browning poem "A Grammarian's Funeral" is at once castigated and extolled: *This man decided not to live but know.*

He has occupied his business in dark cloisters, always solitary, battening tirelessly on other men's leavings, searching among the singular things that he has learned for some animating coherence, some pattern, some fresh provocation to an unimagined epiphany that may itself be stored up, puzzled over, perhaps communicated to another scholar. He has had his use in the world, no doubt, and he always will; but that use, for our purposes, may not be what he thinks it is. In filling the ranks of our first cadre of professors and mentors, I want to hire some like him, less for their substantive academic contributions than for the purity of their answer to their vocations. This lived academic integrity and the quiet, gentle grandeur of character that can be its accompaniment will serve to instruct and to inspire our students, and in ways they will remember in another age, perhaps upon another shore.

Such learned persons, a few perhaps, will hold honored places in the College. But mainly I aim for the school to find and retain men and women who want to teach and to lead and to live among our students. For the young crave such leadership. They are not getting it in our country, upon our campuses— and have not been for half a century. They need it, and, having done without it, most don't know they need it. So that our search must be for those drawn to teaching even before they are drawn to scholarship, to leading before criticizing—for versatile people in whom the effects of their own educations are seen rather than propounded.

I think that the means by which most colleges seek out and hire professors has but the most marginal, accidental link to what sorts of teachers and leaders of undergraduates they are likely to be. Indeed it *is* possible to be a productive scholar and a devoted presence in the lives of students at the same time: to know *and* to live. Who has not himself known these happy few? The enthusiasm of their commitment to their craft is forcibly communicated in the integrity of their scholarship, in the uncompromising character of the standards on which they insist, in the patience and deliberation they bring to every encounter with a student who has sought them out, and in the plain relish with which they greet some success of a much-loved pupil "outside the classroom." Alas, however, by far the greater number of those drawn to research and scholarship will have demonstrated neither aptitude for, nor interest in, going regularly among the young people that they have been asked to teach. On the contrary, they often instruct as though they expected their students themselves to cherish ambitions to become doctors of their own disciplines, rather than executives, architects, businessmen, soldiers, lawyers. Their object should be the animation of intellectual curiosity, the quickening of what will become a self-sustaining and self-disciplined intellectual.

The way to make a young person fall in love with literature, so that his devotion to letters may become the avocation of a lifetime, is not to deconstruct, to belittle, to murder to dissect— before a roomful of thirsty undergraduates; it is to transmit an abiding love and admiration for the best things we teach. At the same time, our professors must assure students grasp the *principle* and form the *habit* of disinterestedness, of rendering judgments that are determinedly impartial, based on evidences and deliberation tenaciously sought and patiently sustained. The weary sarcasms and condescensions of professors bored by "having to teach" undergraduates may be relied upon to do great if unmeasurable damage. One remembers with perfect clarity students of his own day, exclaiming happily over some novel of Wolfe or Cooper, or a history of Barbara Tuchman—only to have the enthusiasm dismissed by the hyperlearned professor nettled by undergraduate enthusiasm.

"What do you teach?" The answer should be: "I teach men and women."

General: The Faculty of the College

The faculty should number about a hundred. Of these, about seventy-five will be designated as "mentors"; the remainder, professors. To serve the needs of our academic work, a total of ten to fifteen mentors and professors *together* will be assigned duties in each of our eight functional academic fields, as we have defined them—mathematics; philosophy; rhetoric and composition; and so on. Some groups will be larger than others, of course—history, for example.

Our teachers will not be organized into university departments; their members will have no "ranks"; and there will be no tenure—which no capable person requires.

"Wretched little nurseries of unceasing discord"—Hamilton's judgment in *Federalist* #9 on the selfish sovereignties that were the American states under the Articles of Confederation—perfectly suits the culture of academic departments in many of our best universities, where the ideals of education are displaced by an avid, self-absorbed quest for administrative power (such as it is).

Our aim must be to recruit and retain mentors and professors whose emotional loyalties remain first to the mission of the College; second, barely, to their students; third, to their academic specialties. There must be a corporate élan, an esprit *common to all*: something like that, for example, of a British regiment or of the Benedictine Order. Professional satisfactions, emphatically, will not derive from promotion or celebrity; rather, from contributing to, and watching the growth in intellectual stature and competence of, our undergraduates.

The distinction between "professor" and "mentor" is basic, and I should describe it now, before moving on to a more detailed consideration of the duties of each of these two classes.

It is partly the distinction between intellectuals who are ordinarily amateurs of their academic disciplines, and learned scholars and teachers who have made their professional lives in such work. It is, partly and generally, a distinction in age—our mentors as a group will be a good deal younger than most of our professors. It is—again with certain exceptions—a distinction between temperaments: to some extent between lives lived according to active, as opposed to contemplative and reclusive, callings. It is most fundamentally a distinction between the missions the College will assign each class of teachers.

Mentors will have variegated responsibilities at the College; professors much more restricted (though surely no less important) ones. Mentors will spend more time in direct work with our students—much of it in venues other than academic ones. The majority of mentors will live in the houses in each of the four villages. The role of professors at the College will be frankly academic, rarely administrative: they will not be asked to dissipate their energies in what is called committee work or in the other collateral duties by which too many able older professors (to borrow a phrase from S. Paige) "angry up the blood" in petty matters of academic contention.

No. For our professors we want to find active scholars who are not active careerists. I do not want to be told that candidate-professor Jones has published twenty books, and then find that they are impenetrable to the honest efforts of ordinary, intelligent laymen (that is, disinterested American citizens). I want, emphatically, men and women who have not been unafraid to tackle the large issues in their disciplines, and who are committed to communicating their conclusions and arguments to lay citizens as well as to other scholars. The work of some scientists and mathematicians apart, I do not believe that academic intellectuals of the first rank cannot write serviceable, graceful prose accessible to all self-educating persons. On the contrary, I regard their ability to do so as a useful test as to whether they themselves understand what they are talking about. To explain something complicated to someone whose prior knowledge of your subject is strictly limited demands that you organize your own analyses and conclusions in an orderly way, and that you communicate their fruits in limpid, engaging prose.

Our professors must have earned reputations as strong teachers. By "strong," I do not mean "entertaining," either, because there are few things more compelling than the communicated integrity of a mind that has mastered the subject on which it discourses—whether we would call that mind "entertaining" or not. Equally, we must insist on retaining professors whom a lifetime of scholarship and teaching has left unjaded, whose capacities for wonder, for delight in the discoveries and inventions of others, are communicable to idealistic young students. To have preserved intact this capacity for a wonder that is childlike and with it the unhesitating generosity of spirit that rejoices in things suddenly *known*, rather than a captious jealousy of their new discoverer—surely these must be prerequisites to great college teaching. As to their "characters," to use the word in a different sense from how we have used it before, I do not care. Kindly or curmudgeonly, demanding or patient, they will find a continuing welcome among our friends at the College so long as they have integrity of mind, devotion to their pupils and to the mission of the College. We will return to their duties momentarily.

Mentors

We must find and hire as mentors men and women who have lived and served other vocations and professions before deciding to do the kinds of things that the College will ask of them. No serious MBA program nowadays admits twenty-one-year-old graduates with new B.A.s; all require students who have "worked" for several years, whose talents and ambitions and expertises have been tested by the frustrations, competition, and demands of the business world. Surely those who are to become teachers in our College, serving as mentors, require such life experiences even more than an ordinary matriculant to an MBA program. They need it as surely as Brahms needed his sessions at a spinet in a waterfront tavern or Conrad his months in the tropics on a rusty steamer. In truth, those who in late adolescence form an ambition to become college professors—at least of the humanities—are *precisely* those who need a few years away from books, professors, laboratories, and reclusive lucubrations. Thus are true vocations answered or rejected or—in the phrase of the diplomat Harold Nicholson—pruned to greater florescence. The captain of Hampshire grenadiers was not without his use to the historian of the Roman Empire.

We must describe their duties:

First, they will offer tutorial instruction in the functional disciplinary area to which they are assigned, and they will lead or moderate seminars in that area as well.

Second, they will be assigned at least one principal collateral duty in the College, and one minor duty. A mentor whose academic responsibility is in Greek and Latin, for example, might also be assigned to a mountaineering team, and might concurrently serve as an advisor to a student organization considering aspects of contemporary drug policy.

Third, they will live in student houses in the villages, in apartments configured to afford comfortable and constant discourse with students who want or need it. Ordinarily they will give their tutorials in the studies of their apartments—and they may take pupils sent them from other villages within the College.

Fourth, each mentor will have primary responsibility for about twenty individual students, four from each cohort, normally students of his own village. For these students he will be the principal mentor, evaluator, and academic advisor. It would be through him, for example, that most College evaluations would be presented. He would be the person to whom required annual memorizations are recited. He would be the College's principal avenue of communication during the student's times away from the demesne. He would be older friend, companion, advisor, mentor—in a relationship that should extend far beyond the years of both upon the demesne.

Mentors must embody the qualities of character we wish to educe in our students. When we say "educe," we mean draw forth... be paragons of the sort of excellence we want our students to learn. And not only to learn, but to become. By "paragon" the College does not mean perfect embodiment or Platonic exemplar; rather, we intend that our mentors provide living testimony to the kind of virtue, the excellence of lives, that we must champion. These men and women, *these mentors, are themselves unfinished persons.* They are to be strivers, searchers, tenaciously engaged in their work. They teach an academic discipline; they live among our students, in the student villages; they serve in a variety of other assignments. These assignments can range from giving music lessons, to serving as part-time coaches or advisors to student organizations, to leading Treks. The point is that their lives and our students' lives intersect constantly, and the enthusiasm and determination of *their* engagement are directly communicated to the students—in the best and most permanent way possible: by the power of example. The mentors more than any other group within the College will inflect and sustain its culture, its *ethos.* Though several faiths will no doubt be represented among our mentors and students, John Winthrop's ardent Christian counsel seems acutely pertinent: "That which the most in their churches maintain as a truth in profession only, we must bring into familiar and constant practice: as in this duty of love we must love brotherly without dissimulation... we must bear one another's burdens."

So that in our selection of mentors we must value, higher than anything else, how the candidates have lived their own lives, and whether those qualities will translate well into the communitarian life of each student village. I need scarcely assert that we are looking for well-educated men and women of action, rather than professional scholars and pedagogues. In our selections we will look hard for evidences of engaged, unsparing, selfless work and service in whatever jobs our candidates have served since taking their own bachelor's, or further, degrees. We should have a certain bias in favor of those who are known to have performed acts of physical bravery or singular moral courage. As Seneca said:

> Certain acts of generosity or humanity or courage have amazed us. We began to admire them as though they were perfect.... From such deeds... we have derived the idea of a good of great magnitude.... We saw someone... who was kindly to his friends, forebearing to his enemies, dutiful and pious in his public and private behavior.... Moreover he was always the same and consistent with himself in every action, good not through policy but under the direction of a character such that he could not only act rightly but could not act without acting rightly. We perceived that in him virtue was perfected. We divided virtue into parts: the obligation of curbing desires, checking fears, foreseeing what has to be done, dispensing what has to be given. We grasped moderation, courage, prudence, justice, and gave to each its due. From whom then did we perceive virtue? That man's orderliness revealed it to us, his seemliness, consistency, the mutual harmony of all his actions, and his great capacity to surmount everything. From this we perceived that happy life which flows on smoothly, complete in its own self-mastery.

In services at the College chapel, among the great texts which should be preached at least once annually are the well-loved verses from Chapter Four of Paul's letter to the Philippians. It may be taken as a perfect Christian counterpoint to

Seneca's *Sentences*: "Finally brethren, whatsoever things are true, whatsoever things are honorable, whatsoever things are just, whatsoever things are pure, whatsoever things are lovely, whatsoever things are gracious, if there is any virtue, if there is any praise, think on these things."

I know we can find some seventy-five such persons in our country—and perhaps a few from abroad, given the heavy language requirements in our curriculum.

Finding Mentors

We must search as vigorously—and as imaginatively—for our mentors as for our pupils.

The College should advertise these positions nationally. We will require a large group of applicants from which to select those best suited to our needs. Our search should be made known on the Internet and in general national publications, especially those that are read in the remote parts of our country, those outside the *zeitungsgebeits* of influential newspapers. Candidates should be drawn from a deep reservoir of talent and aptitudes of the kind we need. Within that reservoir, in the most obscure crevices and hidden springs, we may find our best men and women.

We are no doubt looking for singular people: persons drawn equally by active and contemplative vocations, who move easily and instinctively from places of responsibility and danger to situations of sustained reflection to those of leadership and back again. All will have shown some mastery of at least one aspect of our curriculum. Some will be practitioners of their professed disciplines; others will be theoreticians. Some will be relatively young (say, twenty-eight or thirty); others will be finishing a long tenure in the armed services, foreign service, or government, or completing careers in industry. We will of course insist that no mentor (or professor, for that matter) be appointed who has not worked outside his field of academic research and pedagogy for several years. Emphatically, we do not want young scholars who have moved directly from the B.A. into a graduate program that has led directly to the Ph.D., without working at something else.

We might even seek out a certain cussedness. We should look hard at professors recently denied tenure. Here we will no doubt find some of the men and women we want. Invariably, many are celebrated for their devotion to teaching, to working with the young, and so on, while their absence of scholarly publication is, not too convincingly, lamented. Study how each has conducted himself after this nasty career disappointment.

We should be alert, in searching, for candidates who have finally indulged an abiding avocational passion, perhaps after an active career in an adjoining profession. "All my life I have wanted to...." Who cannot think of such people? Common to those who interest us, however, must be candidates at the center of whose avocation must be—also—an itch, a penchant, a positive passion, to *teach* it. Not only to learn, but to propagate the best that has been said and thought in the world.

I know the process of searching will be tedious and expensive. But if we do not find those best suited to these unusual responsibilities, then we will have been faithless to the mission we have set for ourselves in the first place. Conventional testimonials, refulgent *curricula vitae*, and the like, are of no real use to us, beyond their enumeration of basic qualifications, circumstances of education, and so on. We will need to learn about and to know the candidates personally. All in whom we are truly interested must be brought to the demesne for a time, both to judge their responses to it and to the work we will ask of them, and for us simply to talk with them, for a long time, about the work we are taking in hand. We stress again that what in most colleges is regarded as collateral duty is for us as urgent as the academic or intellectual duties the mentors will undertake, in their responsibilities as academic tutors, moderators of seminars, and indeed classroom teachers: *Do they have a clear, persistent vocation to teach and to serve the young?* Just as the best writers are men and women who have not hung around university English departments, but who have earned their accolades after lives spent in a thousand venues, most as far as possible from citadels of intellect, so too will our best mentors have been those who have known and lived in the world's fight, and made their contributions to it, been among its doughty participants, rather than those who have shunned or hidden from its challenges.

Professors

Each of the eight functional academic areas, as we have defined them, should be led and served by two (and sometimes by three or four) professors. These men and women are to bring to our enterprise both the wisdom and the demonstrated selfless engagement, at the service of that wisdom, that a long professional lifetime of reflection and writing and teaching has wrought in them. Hence their duties: to define syllabi, always with conscious solicitude for the larger mission of the College; to measure students' progress; to supervise the academic work of our mentors; and to lecture the general College as appropriate on important issues touching their discipline. All professors and their families will live on the demesne. Those professors who live in the village houses must, as noted, be carefully selected, since they will be a long-standing presence in the houses. Professors who do not live in the houses will live in or around the villages. I see much of the professors' teaching and study as taking place in the various academic buildings in the Forum. Like our president and our mentors, professors must be convinced adherents of the College's *ethos* and its central purposes, understanding that all elements of our work must conspire in the effort to fulfill our mission: the character of our communal lives, our academic curriculum, and the responsibilities of students outside the obligations imposed by that curriculum.

Scholarship and learnedness shall, in a reciprocity with keen and avid intellects, have made them wise leaders, counselors, eloquent teachers. They will not be self-absorbed drones determined to advance themselves by the production of testimonials to academic dutifulness—so-called learned articles in journals of interest only to other scholars, written in the weary elegances of academic Chinese. In our most important study and largest academic enterprise, for example, we will want historians, not antiquarians. They shall have anyhow been drawn primarily to the teaching of ardent undergraduates, not postgraduate students intending to become professors themselves. Like Cambridge or Oxford dons, or great men like Mark van Doren or Lionel Trilling or C. Vann Woodward, they will have delighted particularly in making plain to intelligent laypersons what seems to them important in the preoccupations of their own fields of interest. And the subjects they will have set for themselves will have been the large ones: was not Trilling's doctoral thesis called, simply, *Matthew Arnold*?

In looking for such people to join our faculty as professors, you should not restrict your searches to the obvious sources: eminent colleges and universities with well-known graduate programs. We want men and women who have been, for many years, devoted and productive scholars. But we want those who have always been known both for their love of teaching and for a certain evangelism in behalf of their disciplines, and within those disciplines. To use examples from our most important field, history: I would hire, if they were still alive, J. W. Wheeler-Bennett or Barbara Tuchman, in a heartbeat; or—and I assume they will still be alive when I am not—John Keegan and David McCullough. Here are absolutely superb historians, deeply and gracefully "scholarly" by any standard, but who have made their lives outside the academy, and who have occasionally been scorned as amateurs, because they have either no scholarly credential or no academic appointment. But what such historians *do* have is something more valuable to our purpose: an instinctive commitment, a compulsion almost, to communicate what they have learned about the past to those who may use it to some purpose other than further scholarship or antiquarian *divertissement*. They are writing for intelligent laypeople, for those who may one day command armies, lead governments and businesses, serve in offices of state, be so situated, that is, that what they have learned will be of some practical use.

The President

Our first on-the-ground leader must be an enthusiastic partisan of the College's purposes and the means by which we propose to achieve them. He is to serve for a maximum of six years, and will not be allowed to succeed himself. Nor is his successor to be drawn from the immediate College faculty—academic or administrative.

As in all such undertakings, the aim here is to find and hire, not the *best* man, but the *right* man. Jimmy Carter, for example, was surely a kind of "best" man—tireless, analytical, moral, patriotic, experienced. He was not, for the American presidency, the *right* man. A half-century ago, a president of Brown told a search committee just organizing itself that it should not be seduced by eager credentials and a "great" reputation. "After all," he said, "he will spend most of his time dedicating garages." Such mordant counsel evokes a memory of the Duke of Wellington, during his time as prime minister. He was asked who should be sent to command a British force attacking Rangoon. "Lord Saye and Sele." "But he is a fool," came the reply. "Yes," said the duke, "but he can take Rangoon." Simply, we want the person aptest for *our* presidency. Presidential searches, like forward passes, lead to three results, two of them bad. The less bad is this: all unite in seeing that the new man is a fool, or that he is completely overwhelmed by his duties. He is easily fired. Much more dangerous is the diligent mediocrity; as in all professions, he presents the most difficult threat to the achievement of his organization's goals. The board is reluctant to fire him. He is a good person (until 1990, or thereabouts, he was called a good man); he surely "means well," and for hard work, well, his predecessor couldn't hold a candle to him. But he is bad at his job. In the circumstances, most boards let him stay on for a decent time—alas, about five years—and then "honor his long-standing desire to return to classroom teaching."

Plainly, we must complete our forward pass. We must first ask ourselves the question all search committees for presidents must ask: *What is the principal need of our College for the next several years?* We should recruit for that need; and if the woman or man we want is best at *that*, then we should not worry about how good she is at addressing need number two or number three.

Only Ted Williams (hitting a pitched baseball and casting a dry fly) could do two things better than anyone else.

Presidential searches fail for the same reason military promotion boards *succeed*, but only in times of peace. They try to find perfectly safe—or, rather, safely perfect—candidates, disqualifying anyone who has risked or failed greatly or who has offended someone by being controversial. The testimonials of what are called distinguished credentials are adduced both at the moment of soliciting nominations and when the appointment of the new president is made, as though such things truly bore testimony to the character and aptitude needed to discharge the responsibilities of the job. It is thought, also, that "the faculty will be angry if we don't hire an academic" (Ph.D., widely published, tenured faculty member, and so on); and it is urged that every constituency of the college be represented in the "selection process."

But this is not always useful. If the views of all are to be weighed equally, it is foolish. If they are not to be weighed equally, the groups that do not get their way will account themselves cynically manipulated, sandbagged. "Why did you ask us if you weren't interested in what we had to say?"

We want and need someone who in his character and life stands for the things the College will strive to inculcate, to teach, and to assure our pupils learn to teach themselves. I do not hesitate to invoke the familiar distinction between leaders and managers. It is pertinent here. Our conviction is that we teach and lead (again, for the purpose of *our* College) more by who we are, by how we live our lives, than by what we profess.

This both complicates and simplifies our job. First, we will not "announce" a search; I am not interested in people who want to be presidents of colleges. Further, although our man or woman must lead and help administer the College, he will have no development duties and no state legislature to preoccupy and deflect his energies. He will, of course, teach; and he will surely throw himself into many of the challenges he will set before his students. We should be looking at (or rather for) candidates who have set themselves difficult goals, who have persisted for some years until they have achieved those goals, who have had at least one big failure or severe professional disappointment in their lives, who have been indifferent to the blandishments of material success, and who are both quiet and not terribly introspective. I also think that, given the care and imagination that we will bring to the effort, we can find such a person who is both firm in conviction and of a conciliating disposition. I don't want a bastard or a tyrant. *Suaviter in modo, fortiter in re.*

Western history—the study of its great men and women whose lives inspire, chasten, and instruct—is at the core of our curriculum. The emulation they inspire will receive powerful, daily corroboration and reinforcement, by our example, and especially the example of the College's president. The "dailiness," if I may so call it, is urgent: students must see and hear all of what his leadership gives them, not just speeches or announcements or, God cast me down for employing the revolting word, visibility.

Remembering that the mission of the College is to prepare our students to give virtuous and disinterested service and leadership to the Republic, we remind ourselves that we must ask precisely such things of the president of our College and indeed of certain other leaders in our community. We must have a man of versatility easily and unself-consciously borne, neither scholar nor ambitious executive, nor—God again forbid—"consensus builder," but a leader whose life is testimony to his convictions and *ethos*, and whose convictions are the ones that we want our students to cherish. He would probably have served a number of years in the military or in government (not necessarily at the federal level). His reputation for integrity and disinterest must be sterling. Again I would hope that we can find someone who has publicly fallen on his sword once or twice, on behalf of something in which he deeply believes, and about which he risked a great deal. We especially need a man drawn to the young.

Our first president will have a determinative influence on the course of events at the College. I do not want him to be what is called a genius, or what passes for genius, in a Robert Maynard Hutchins sort of way. Its standard presentation is a kind of persuasive volubility, tricked out with *mondain* allusions, foundation mumbo-jumbo, dropped names, and the polished parlor-trick skill of making multiple dependent clauses parse neatly at the end of long sentences. Businessmen are impressed by such a package, and that both depresses me and reminds me that their liberal education has failed them.

Steadiness of belief, determination, patience, communicable relish for the task and great love for the College—these, and a merely good mind, are what I am after. Last, the first president must have the skill, undoubtedly crucial at the start of our community, of identifying, persuading, hiring, and sustaining very good people for the College. He will have to be his own search firm, for there is no such outfit, that I know of, that I would entrust with finding men and women for such an institution as ours.

Succeeding presidents should be the choice of the alumni of the College, who will understand plainly what the office of president requires in its incumbents—not an "administrator," but a leader. For the record, I think these leaders might be found in the ranks of captains of line naval vessels, headmasters of remote New England boarding schools, abbots in Benedictine monasteries, ambassadors to troubled Third World countries. When the alumni look for leaders, I trust they will look at such as these. Such people often have the heart, temperament, courage, and conviction we will need in our president—and for that matter in the masters of the four College villages. Obviously we want lively and well-furnished minds who have considered how their own education, for good or for ill, has influenced their lives. I like also the prize awarded the young Charles de Gaulle by his school: "For Demonstrated Resistance to Fatigue."

Second-ranking billets in universities and colleges are not normally sources for the kinds of leaders we want. These jobs, attractive to the weary and not infrequently ambitious, stifle, rather than cultivate, the qualities we need.

Administration

We have presumed to describe those things that might make a useful president for the College, and pointed toward sources of candidates for the job. As to the administration itself, I am chary of setting down expectations that, in their failure to anticipate certain challenges to be answered and obstacles to be overcome, may prove either irrelevant or indeed perhaps harmful. What is wanted is an administration of condign capability; no more, no less. It would be idle not to recognize that some effort will be needed to administer the various, and usual, programs the College will maintain, *viz*, especially, those that will connect our students with their interim obligations and arrange their terms abroad for language study—and indeed their year in military service.

A few observations and suggestions nonetheless:

1. Everyone who helps administer the College must be a teacher. All must take their places regularly in tutorial instruction, the leading and moderating of seminars, in refectory meal readings, and lectures. It should be understood that administrators serve fixed terms, after which they will return to academic and pedagogical duties. They will live in and around the villages and Forum and be fully engaged in the life of the College.

2. There is to be no "administration building." Like the "computer buildings" of the 1970s, such places house contemporary dinosaurs: huge and ponderous equipments that do little but keep leaders out of touch with those they are charged to lead, or to help. Rather, the various administrative duties are to be—quite literally—spread among and around the various buildings in the Forum or in the villages themselves. An efficient business officer, for example, needs only his laptop and printer, his modem and fax, to discharge his duties; and better when meetings are needed to have them in assembly rooms near the village refectories than in an "administration building" on the central campus. The president himself should attach himself during the academic terms to the different villages, or, occasionally, hang his hat in the fine arts building or library. If the founders and leaders of the largest American corporations can transact business in a diner, and if Abraham Lincoln could proudly say that a man's hat is his office,

then our president can do without the usual pompous equipages and portly ornate barricades of antechambers, offices, secretarial platoons, and the like. I cannot forbear adding that, since the raising of monies will form no part of the president's duty, he will not have to "entertain" in order to extract those monies.

I should perhaps add here that the College will not bestow honorary degrees. Long ago such places as the Virginia Military Institute and the University of Virginia decided that transparent condescensions like these would invariably confound and conflate genuine achievement with political opportunism—the school's self-regarding opportunism, that is—both cheapening the honorific and exciting, among papabili, an unseemly desire for such recognition.

3. There is a corollary, in academic bureaucracy, to Parkinson's Law—the law that holds that work expands so as to fill the time available for it. That corollary is that administration grows so as to create more work for administration to do.

But not here, not in our College.

The Board of Trustees

Our small, five-member board, Robert, now includes you, a second lawyer, my successor at the company, a Wyoming rancher called Horton with whom I went to college, and a teacher from Santa Fe. I cannot prescribe how this small kitchen cabinet may evolve, but I have an idea how it *should* evolve, and what—as it becomes a real "board"—its mission should be. Like the present group, most plainly, it must be united in its zeal for the task, its sustaining loyalty to the mission of the

College, and its connatural wisdom in making judgments about character—the character of those who will lead the College. Emphatically, the board should be a working board: well informed, faithful in discharging obligations, enthusiastic in its evangelism for the school, and, when possible, able to do us some real good. A good size for the board, I think, is about ten.

I have served on the boards of three universities or schools. Scott Fitzgerald warned: Start with an individual and you have a type; start with a type and you have... nothing. But I will take the risk. There are three types of trustees, and I have seen plenty of exemplars of each—on the boards of private and state schools both.

The first, and by far the most common, type is an able person who is sought out for his energy, for (what is called) visibility, for clear and strong links to the college, and for his willingness either to give or to raise money. On the whole he is an admirable man. He is also busy, much engaged in the business of busyness, quite clubbable, fairly (but not completely) reliable in discharging board and committee duties. He often reads his board papers on the plane en route to meetings, and misses one of every five of these assemblies (having faithfully called the chairman, who, quick to "take" the call, felicitates the trustee on his refreshing candor and says that the board will miss his counsel). This trustee is on several other boards, some *pro bono*, some not; is in his fifties; has a thousand other obligations; and wants to be helpful—and will be, if he is needled and petted. Boards that have a provision for a one-year hiatus between trustee terms turn such trustees over with a proper aplomb, imagining that their successors will be more attentive and committed. Some will, most will not. The one thing that such trustees may offer is sound judgment about the college's leadership, and if they do, their appointments may be justifiable, on this ground alone.

The second category, perhaps ten or fifteen percent of the whole, comprises ornamental or political people, such appointments made without reference to what kinds of trustees the new persons are likely to be. A thousand-year-old name, a putative link to a family fortune, an echoey presence connected to a great athletic memory, a disappointed aspiration to some higher government honorific—it is all the same. Such trustees are faithful in their attendance at meetings (in my view one of the least important criteria in assessing the usefulness of trustees), silent or uninformed in counsel, hearty in displaying their appointment in resumés and the like, awkward in the extreme in committee work that brings them face-to-face with students or professors.

On a board of average size for an American university—let us say, twenty—we are fortunate indeed if we find five members of our last type or category; namely, trustees whose enthusiasm for the work, whose readiness and wisdom in counsel, whose disinterested willingness to do what they think is needed, or what is asked of them, is constant and positive inspiration. Such trustees are those for whom their commitment to the institution is the overriding civic, *pro bono* commitment of their lives. They are so determined to be helpful that we are inspired by them. Ordinarily, also, they will not themselves have been particularly strong scholars, long ago, while they were undergraduates; so that they have a certain diffidence, becoming and admirable, in pressing their views or visions of what the school should be doing. And as men and women who have made a success of their lives in the world of affairs they are sensitive to the needed prerogatives of faculty and administration. They keep their nose in, and their hands out—in the old, not completely felicitous aphorism about good trusteeship. My own experience leads me to note that most of this group are people recently retired from business or government, who have time and energy to devote to trusteeship, and who in the springtime of their senility bring a fresh and radiant enthusiasm to the work.

For our own venture I would be inclined again to repeat Eisenhower's advice at Columbia. Responding to a question about where a sidewalk should be laid down, he is supposed to have told the questioner to watch where the students walk for a couple of years—and put it there. In other words, let my private foundation trustees sustain the venture in its earliest days; let them decide on the best ways to find and retain their own successors, set the length of terms, and so on.

These observations are bland and unexceptionable. But I have two others to make. First, every trustee is to live at the College for two weeks each year, in one of the residential villages, and to make one Trek with students. While living in the village, in the guest quarters of one of the houses, it should be understood that his apartment is to be open to students and mentors alike for discussions about College issues or general conversation. He will take his meals in the village refectory. The less time he spends with those called "administrators," the better: *not* because he cannot learn from them or should not understand their problems and aspirations, but because time so spent removes him from useful learning about what is really taking place at the school, and what should be. It removes him from what really matters—our students.

Second—and here we recur to a continuing theme—in these ruminations, he (or she) is to be the kind of person who has tried to live a life of virtuous and disinterested citizenship, and whose character and ability have led him to positions of leadership and responsibility. In the versatility and range of his interests, he palpably embodies the best features of both active and contemplative vocations—recalling, if it is not too much to say, the unconscious versatility of the Founders of our country, moving easily and happily from the study to the Congress to the work of his profession to such enterprises as will contribute usefully to the common good. And when there is praise to be offered, or honors to be conferred upon him, he is not present.

Finally, as to term of appointment. The trustee is to have an unlimited number of four-year terms, each, however, separated from the previous one by a required "sabbatical" of one year. This seems to me ideal. Those who are not good trustees are thanked properly if a trifle disingenuously after their four-year stint, and allowed to disappear either without a trace or with some sense of usefulness; the others are in effect kept in the enterprise during their year "off," and reappointed to continue their useful services.

There should, of course, always be a trustee or two from Wyoming. The board should also be conscious that our studentry is a national one, and that all students will be required to live and study abroad for a term. It may be useful to seek out and invite onto the board trustees from the countries in which our students are living.

I expect the board to assure that the endowment is managed prudently and imaginatively, so that its growth may be sustained while the income it produces remains adequate to the uses for which it is being designated. Above all the board is to maintain an energetic solicitude for the College's capability to defray all costs incident to our students' education at the College—their tuition and all ancillary fees. Someday the budget will come under pressure, and there will be an outcry that the College should eliminate the subvention for rich students. I do not want this done. All are to attend without fee. Merit is the only criterion for admission and continuing enrollment—merit as defined and measured as we have stated previously.

I expect the board to find, hire, support, advise, evaluate, and—when necessary—fire the president.

I expect that the board will insist that the president and faculty, in making judgments about whom to enroll, and whom to hire to teach, weigh equally the claims of character and mind; and, in the case of students, I expect the board always to search zealously for clues as to a student's likely fulfillment of the College's ambitions for her, or him, many years hence. What is he likely to be like at fifty?—given the kind of education we are going to provide, and the qualities of character and intellect that we have looked for, in him, when we scrutinized his claims to be admitted? With teachers, mentors and professors both, trustees must assure that a *genuine vocation to teach and to serve students*, and to make decisions with reference exclusively to *their* welfare, be sustained.

The Republic will depend always for its vital and ideal existence upon an educated and virtuous citizenry, one that believes that righteousness exalts a nation. So long as the College adheres to the purpose of preparing its students to take their honored places in this long and noble profession, it will fulfill the mission that I have given it. There is no antipathy between this mission and the traditional aim, or aims, of that form of education commonly called "liberal." On the contrary: they should inform and strengthen one another. Those present at the creation of our country, those who led and made the creation, demonstrated that those of large intellectual endowment—always energetically, buoyantly cultivated—were often to the fore in serving missions and offices that demanded raw courage moral and physical, selfless hardihood, and tenacity of purpose: the whole laid before the altar of American honor and freedom.

In the selection of those we will ask to serve and to lead the College, we must be bound by the evidences of how candidates have lived their own lives, what has been of value to them, and what those evidences suggest about their fitness to live in the communitarian mode, however it may evolve, of our school. We must look for abundant evidences of engaged, unsparing, and selfless work and service in whatever jobs our candidates have served. We should have a certain bias in favor of those who have (1) performed acts of physical bravery, (2) demonstrated moral courage by standing up for unpopular positions or convictions, and (3) been notably magnanimous, after intense disagreement or dispute, toward political or business foes. I must be forgiven for speaking in the first person, but I am sick unto death (indeed) at the viciousness, the intemperance, the settled rancor that subsists among men and women who have chosen to make their living as professors and administrators in universities; and at the absence of an engaged discourse in which adversaries on campuses listen to each other, in which they impute good will to their opponents, and in which both sides enter with the clear sense that each can learn from the other.

The powerful harmony of an ancient litany will have been heard in the lives of those we will appoint, as it will one day be heard in the lives of those who will be our students. It is a harmony that unites legacies both classical and Christian, both yet resonating in the hearts of many of our countrymen. Its early celebrants included the great Stoic philosophers—among them Epictetus, Seneca, Cicero, Marcus Aurelius; among the early Christians, our debt here is greatest to St. Paul. Marcus Aurelius wrote simply what he knew, believed, and lived: "Do not argue about what it means to be a good man. Be one." He understood that the source and sustenance of an engaged life that is also a life of integrity must be the same for all, and that it is best taught through the intercessories of human example. No tribute to a parent is more poignant than his memorial to his adopted father, Antonius Pius, whom the emperor remembered for his "lenience, his firm refusal to be diverted from any decision he had deliberately reached, his complete indifference to meretricious honors; his industry, perseverance, and willingness to listen to any project for the common good...."

Student Obligation Upon Graduation

Each new graduate will serve, in some agency of government, for a minimum of three years, this obligation to be discharged not more than five years from the date of the award of the diploma and degree from the College. Military service and public school teaching will satisfy the obligation, provided the graduate serves three consecutive years in these fields. Reserve military service, or substitute teaching, or teaching while in full-time pursuit of advanced degrees, will not serve to discharge the obligation.

Dear Robert,

As my mind becomes more and more shrouded by the fog of the war that is fought within me, I find that often the only thing that can restore my mind to focus are the lines I memorized in my youth. We must ensure that our own students, in similar extremities, might find solace, comfort, instruction, and discipline from similar—or the same—lines, and not from commercial jingles. Therefore, I remind you that students at the College are to commit two thousand lines to memory each academic year. They should recite these lines before their principal mentors, in increments of not less than two hundred—such recitations to be given whenever students choose and mentors are available. My "lines" embrace lines from poetry, speeches, plays, works of philosophy, history, literature. The College should particularly encourage the memorization of poetry from foreign languages. Any lines approved by principal tutors are to be allowed.

No doubt this is a startling and singular requirement. But there are good reasons for it.

The first is disciplinary. Both definitions of "discipline" are useful in explaining our purpose. First, that of making a sustained solitary effort to learn something thoroughly—and learning as prerequisite to an enriched understanding. Second, as an exercise in concentration: in setting the mind to labor at a worthy task, in an activity quite uncongenial to the present age, and, one does not doubt, to future ages.

Second: to learn something that is exquisite, to know "the best that has been said and thought in the world," not only so that it may be lodged in our minds forever, and that therefore it will be there always to instruct us, but also that it may serve as Matthew Arnold might acknowledge it to be: a touchstone, a classic that has survived because it has spoken directly to succeeding generations.

Third: to know such lines over a lifetime is to know them differently; they swim unbidden into our consciousness, simply because we are not the same men and women that we were when we learned those lines twenty or ten years ago. Passages that we know in the telling phrase, "by heart," suddenly irradiate the mind, evoked by the plangency of scent, sight, sound.

We know them sometimes almost as if we had not known them before.

Memory in the young is ample and elastic, almost limitlessly so. The most difficult lines to learn are committed to young minds with relative ease.

One's own experience seems pertinent. It was not until I had known Hopkins's poem "Pied Beauty" for ten years that I understood its message was a message of searching, active toleration for the disregarded, the eccentric, and the unusual; nor until I had committed to my memory the second paragraph of Lincoln's Second Inaugural that I grasped its elements in their completeness; nor until I had memorized Lee's Farewell to the Army of Northern Virginia and known it for thirty years that I understood why Lee was so great a man, so great an American, as well as so brilliant a general and leader of men.

The minds and memories of our public people seem empty of those things that might serve them well as even the most austere furniture of metaphor, reference, illuminating example. It is as though our leaders, though they might acknowledge that "I majored in English and philosophy in college," remember none of what they once knew, not even the loveliest and most moving of passages. And as for adding to whatever meager stock of such furniture they took with them from their formal educations—it is a demonstrated certainty that they have not done so.

Yours,
John Adams

*A*DAMS KEPT BOTH JOURNALS *and commonplace books. He noted poems and excerpts from histories, speeches, novels, documents, that gave him particular pleasure, and wrote MEM next to some of them. Given the College's determination to require two thousand lines of memorization of every student, each year, it seems appropriate to include a few of these among those items for memorization set by the faculty. Books furnish a room; lines committed to memory help furnish a mind. As Adams noted in his small memorandum on memorization, those things that are exquisite, and that we have in our minds, will appear in fresh and vivid lineaments when, at different times in our lives, they spring to our mind—provoked by thousands of circumstances, unbidden certainly. We know them again for the first time.*

1. *"Ulysses"—Tennyson*
2. *"Ithaca"—Cavafy*
3. *Polonius to Laertes—Shakespeare*
4. *"If"—Kipling*
5. *Howard Moss: "The Gift to Be Simple"*
6. *Abraham Lincoln: Second Inaugural Address*
7. *Abraham Lincoln: Letter to General Joseph Hooker, January 1863*
8. The Autobiography of Edward Gibbon, *passim*
9. *Lee's Farewell to the Army of Northern Virginia*
10. *"Horatius at the Bridge," from Lord Macaulay's* Lays of Ancient Rome

—R.P.

CHAPTER 7

Postmortem

[The following letter is Adams's last to me. Perhaps his mind was "going" at last. The thoughts don't track, but the observations are still acute.

I learned Mr. Adams had died two days after I received the letter, and with it, the citation from Psalm 71. R.P.]

M Y DEAR ROBERT,

"These things," wrote Marcus Aurelius, "I learned from my father. Strength, steadfastness, and moderation on all occasions, a spirit perfectly balanced and indomitable, like the one he showed during the illness which took him away." The father is supposed to have murmured "*aequanimitas*" just before he died: *equanimity.*

I wonder what Antoninus died of? Not, surely, metasta-sized prostatic cancer. We imagine the classical great to have lain quietly down, in their robes, and to have subsided. Or, like Cato of Utica, to have died by their own hands, for a principle. But I (that am not shaped for sportive tricks...), I am on a new, and—it would appear—final, protocol, basically a drug called Oxycontin. This is sustained-release morphine sulphate, the drug itself handsomely reinforced during spikes of pain by Roxanol. A gooey decoction that hastens total relief. Partly as a consequence I feel myself going cloudy again, from time to time, my thoughts unlinking and floating, almost like those trailers pulled through the summer skies by biplanes, with curt slogans or instructions on them: *Buy Gillette.* Please forgive me. I have won through to a kind of equanimity, but it is drug-assisted. I am no better than an East German swimmer on a sustaining diet of steroids, you might say.

Not to sound apocalyptic. But if I cannot write more, as I intended to, on memorization, let me fling down a few items as they float into my mind: things I want the students to remember because they are exquisite, and because memorizing is good for them and easy for the young, and because, once learned this way, such things will be turned over in the mind again, and again, ten years hence, or fifty, and they will know the things suddenly as they did not know them before. Chapter V, Section II, the *Constitution of the Commonwealth of Massachusetts*. The first John Adams at his shining, bumptious best. Cohort I should be made to learn it during their first August orientation, the section that begins, "Wisdom and knowledge, as well as virtue, diffused generally among the body of the people, being necessary for the preservation of their rights and liberties." And ends in a glorious laundry list: "…general benevolence, public and private charity, industry and frugality, honesty and punctuality in their dealings, sincerity, good humor and all social affections…." Good humor, Robert, frugality and punctuality. Does anyone talk of such things any more? On my television, flossy and preening, the lawyer of Monica Lewinsky debouches from his limousine, and is assailed by an *Eyewitness News* team! A feminist sachem reappears to felicitate the president on his response to Just Said No. Punctuality! Good humor!

But the Adams quotations, as above, certainly. The Funeral Address of Pericles: "Fall in love with your city…." Burke's great speech to the Electors of Bristol. Patrick Henry in St. John's Church. Washington to his officers at Newburgh. Jefferson's First Inaugural Address; Robert E. Lee's Farewell to the Army of Northern Virginia; Lincoln's letters to Joseph Hooker and to Mrs. Bixby; the Gettysburg Address and the penultimate paragraph of the Second Inaugural; FDR's Four Freedoms; the Kennedy Inaugural, at which I was present, a speech that will endure, I am sure: it is almost like the first line of a novel, the last page of which is the lift-off of the last American chopper from the roof of the embassy in Saigon.

"Western Wind." Keats's "Standing Aloof in Giant Ignorance." Wordworth's "Westminster Bridge" and "Tintern Abbey." Macaulay's *Lays of Ancient Rome.* "Ozymandias"—nothing beside remains; round the decay of that colossal wreck, boundless and bare, the lone and level sands stretch far away: It is strange how that line evokes perfect silence and a stilling of the wind, as, each morning, just before daybreak, there is a great stillness here on this little corrugation of Wyoming Piedmont.

I am tired and fading. Cavafy, "Ithaca": May your journey be... long: every American ought to have it stapled to his forehead. All the dense middle Hopkins sonnets, hard to commit to memory, but not knowable until done this way, and known for a while. Howard Moss on Einstein: "The Gift to Be Simple...."

Lots of Kipling and Masefield for Cohort I; Longfellow— "Sail On O Union"; Whitman, Poe.

At least one long poem in both foreign languages every student must master.

The Bill of Rights. The Virginia Statute of Religious Freedom. The Declaration.

As I say, cloudy and unlinked. At my left hand lies a medical journal with an essay marked out for me to read, by Dr. deBurgh—the subject is reversed terminal cases involving diffusive metastases. Doctors write like academic literary critics. The ads in the journal are interesting. The Nearly-Old predominate in these glossy four-color frames—bent forward, pain-free but still stiffly recuperative, cherubic grandchildren at their patting hands, wobbling on their trikes. The old folks' faces as compositions of deliberate sweetness.

Pope, the part of the *Essay on Criticism*, in which the words are made to sound the sense that they proclaim and mean.

Robert, thank you for what you are doing for us. May I be precatory with you—to use your good lawyers' word? Somehow honor this wonderful man, our president between the Mighty Eminences of Washington and Jefferson, at the College.

I attach also the Psalm I was reading this morning, not an hour after I wrote the last page of my instructions about the College. You will see the obvious, not to say, eerie, links:

O God, you have taught me since I was young,
And to this day I tell of your wonderful works.
And now that I am old and gray-headed, O God, do not
    forsake me,
Til I make known your strength to this generation
And your power to all who are to come.
Psalm 71

[This was found in John Adams's computer the day after he died—a "fragment" that, perhaps, he was going to use later. R.P.]

I ASKED THAT OUR STUDENTS RESERVE AN HOUR each day for silence and solitude. "We may spare this hour's time, to practice for eternity." In these long, silent night-watches, I have, I suppose, been at practice: not consciously at first, but now, certainly—as you will also have to do. I know well the counsel both of Sophocles ("made this valid law, that man must learn by suffering...") and of Romans. It is singular how each identically insists that suffering instructs, that it fortifies the soul and produces (saith St. Paul) "endurance, and endurance produces character, and character produces hope, and hope does not disappoint us, because God's love has been poured into our hearts." The price, the cost rather, is bitter and squalid; yet I believe that the faith that sustains some of us, and the considered, reasoned life, the life of ceaseless learning and of working somehow to make the counsels of mind superintend the urgings and imperatives of will, of desire, of appetite—that such a life brings one to the final gate with something approaching equanimity and with certitude, even, that much will remain to us when we have crossed over. I must believe that.

Sviatoslav Richter died last year. I heard him when he came to our country in 1960. There has never been a pianist like him. Just before that time he played a concert in Sofia, and a purloined copy of the recording was smuggled out: the *Moussorgsky Pictures at an Exhibition*, the last section of which is called "The Great Gates at Kiev." Every pianist who has ever performed it has thundered out the scene and sound, vehemently bravura, the awful sight uprearing before the traveller. But Richter did it so quietly, so simply, with such unforced calm and restraint, that I suddenly understood the composer's intention, and perhaps the meaning of the scene, as I had not done before. The traveller had come to the Gates in reverence and awe, but composed, calm, certain that he had finally prepared himself, through all the means earned and given him, to pass through.

11 April 1998

DOUGLAS, Wyo. (AP) — John Adams, 71, died yesterday at his ranch near Douglas, Wyoming. Mr. Adams, who had served in the Department of Defense in the Kennedy Administration, was co-founder of the Carswell Corporation in 1974, and, with Robert Carswell, sold the company to CPU Corporation in 1987. He was a graduate of the University of Chicago and served in the Marine Corps in World War II. He won the Navy Cross on Iwo Jima. His foundation, which he created to establish a new college with his accumulated fortune, announced immediately that the college (to open in 2000) will be named for him.

Mr. Adams left no survivors.

Acknowledgments

I WANT TO THANK SEVERAL PEOPLE particularly for their kindnesses and counsel during the writing of this book. My wife, Diana Bunting, has as always been constant, tolerant, and patient in her enthusiasm and support of such undertakings. Harry Crocker, my editor at Regnery, suggested that I write about an ideal college for our time, as John Henry Newman had done for all time. He has been steadfast and generous with his advice and encouragements. Mr. Ward Good was especially helpful in the descriptions of "John Adams's" career. Four Virginia Military Institute (VMI) colleagues have been especially helpful: Brigadier General Alan F. Farrell, for his suggestions and help in preparing the section called "Atonement with the Machine"; Colonels William D. Badgett and Albert L. Deal III, for their suggestions in sections on the fine arts and mathematics; and, finally, Colonel Edwin L. Dooley, Jr., who has been inestimably helpful and constant in the work of preparing the manuscript.

Finally, I must salute and thank the Corps and Faculty of VMI for the continuing chance to live and work among them at a time in American history when the things for which they work are more urgently needed by our country than at any time in the history of this school.

And I wish to thank the following friends, old and new, whose generous counsel, ideas, and items of advice and information were helpful in the preparation of this book. They include many colleagues at VMI.

Dr. G. Whitney Azoy
Roger Barrus
Tina Bennett
Albert J. Beveridge III
Dr. Laurent Boetsch
Dr. Derek Bok
Dr. Eva T.H. Brann
Kevin L. Brown
Willard Bunn III
Colonel Gordon O. Calkins, Jr.
David Cantlay
David L. Copeland, MD
Reverend R. David Cox
Gretel Erlich
Dr. Joseph J. Ellis
Ward Good
Senator Elmon T. Gray
David V. Hicks
Dr. Gertrude Himmelfarb
Lieutenant Colonel
    Janet S. Holly
Bishop and Caroline Hunt
Jay Katzen
George F. Kennan
Colonel A. Cash Koeniger
Ross Mackenzie

Colonel Mike E. Monsour
Kathleen Norris
Dr. Martha Nussbaum
Sister Colman O'Connell,
    O.S.B.
John O'Grady
Chaplain James S. Park
Lori R. Parrent
Dr. Harry C. Payne
Father Paul Philibert, O.P.
Major Duncan Richter
David Riesman
Father Joel Rippinger, O.S.B.
Dr. Sue Ellen Rocovich
Colonel William C. Sauder
Lieutenant Colonel Rose
    Mary Sheldon
Admiral James B. Stockdale
Father Terrence Kardong,
    O.S.B.
Dr. Eduardo A. Velasquez
Joel Wallman
Cadet Jerry B. Webb II
George F. Will
Gabriella F. Youngblood
Lieutenant David W. Zirkle

PS 3552 .U48 E38 1998
Josiah Bunting III
An Education for Our Time